Little RED
THE POWER OF
Transparency

TABLE OF CONTENTS

ACKNOWLEDGMENTS

I have had a team of supporters over the years and it wouldn't be right to not acknowledge their impact:

To my grandparents, thank you for believing in me and supporting me when it felt like no one else did. Gran your amazing, your faith made me strong. Papa, your love made kind.

To my parents, you all did such an amazing job raising me and I thank you for that. You both have shown me to keep striving, Mom your determination made me strive. Dad, your fight helped me win.

We fight, we argue, and we love because that is what siblings do. I couldn't ask for better siblings than you. Reesha, you are the first person to ever show me what loving God was. Mikey, you pushed me to get an education and pass the bar. Marq, being in your presence means more to me than you will ever know.

To my pastors and religious leaders thank you for all that you have done and poured out to me. Apostle and First lady Howard, I will never forget the hours you labored over and with me.

To all those who stepped in when you didn't have to, I ask God to continue to step into your life when he doesn't have to! You are such blessings to me.

To my readers, thank you for taking this journey with Little Red because if it hadn't been for you, we both would have ended our story a long time ago. Much like Red I used to place blame on everyone but myself, but I understand now more than ever that everything truly does happen for a reason. I wouldn't take anything back or ask for a redo because I am who am because of my scars (self-inflicted or not).

LEAVING THE BUBBLE

It was 1996, surprisingly a warm day for Ohio's below freezing winter. Late-December the temperature had rose to 60°F and somehow the day was getting warmer. On the 5th floor of a Metro Health Hospital ; in the delivery rooms it was surprisingly a slow day. Walking down to the incubators you will notice there were only a few new babies added that day. You can even look at the charts this was not a normal day.

I didn't know what was going on that day, I just felt the need to leave. So, I started pushing my way out and my oh my, the walls were caving in on me. For the first time in my 8-month life I did not want to be where I was. It was pretty comfortable for those 8 months, but I just had an instinct that my growth would be limited. I kept hearing voices outside of my bubble. A soft voice murmured before panicking, "she's not supposed to be here for another month! IS MY BABY OKAY?" A deeper voice "Nurse, can you give my wife some drugs? AND WHERE'S THE DOCTOR?" I had been hearing these voices a lot lately.

I was still stuck and I was getting mad! I may have accidentally done some more wiggles, but I kept hearing that soft voice, who calls itself *Mummy loves you*, screaming in fear. I wonder what *Mummy loves you* is. It seems really close to me, sometimes like it's invading my space. I remember when I had discovered movement and I wanted to kick and roll, for some reason it said in agony: "it's time to go to bed sweetie, please!" It's a voice; although it's soft, it is probably the loudest. It's kind of invasive when you're trying to enjoy yourself. I did like bed time though it seemed quieter.

OOOOOOOOH, there's a light at the end of this tunnel thingy, so I try to wiggle some more. But wait, I see these claws and I can't wiggle back. DANG IT! I knew I should have stayed where I was comfortable! The claws are touching me but they don't hurt. I never knew what the end felt like but this wasn't too bad. The claws keep pulling and I feel like I am in a different texture. I can't really explain it but maybe it's, that's it, a quaint voice blurts "Low oxygen levels, heart rate …" I am in low oxygen levels. Still not sure what it is, so I just wait for my end. They pulled me out of my comfort spot and I am consumed in low oxygen levels.

It's not too bad but I liked how I breathed in my bubble. It hurts to breathe in low oxygen levels.

OWWWW! Those claws lied, they do hurt and they hit my booty. I don't think I like this end anymore. So, I insist they put me back in my bubble, but everyone starts clapping like they been waiting on me to talk. They start moving me around and now I am way too far from my bubble. This is what I get for leaving early or at all for that matter. I can't really see much, there are a lot of bright lights, but I keep hearing *Mummy loves you* and *Daddy's here* voice! Those same voices from the bubble, it is kind of reassuring. I was placed on this blob and I don't think the blob knew I was even there but it spoke and said almost in delusion, "I can't doctors, not right now!" It was *Mummy loves you* voice! Poor blob was hurting and I tried to peek my eyes but nothing.

Another blob picked me up with those claws but not to spank me this time. "She's precious, Doctor why is she so yellow?", *Daddy's here* voice said. When I peeked my eyes, I was amazed *Daddy's here* made me feel like a princess. It gave me back to another blob but I felt like I was being tossed, they put me in this new bubble thing and I was happy with my alone time. I learned that some blobs where nurses, doctors, grans, sissy, bubbas, aunties, and uncles. I spent a lot of time with nurses they kept saying they were running test.

My new bubble was kind of shinny and I could see through it. When I looked around, I seen other babies, at least that's what the nurses said we were. My bubble was warm and cozy and occasionally I would get visitors. They were all so sweet. They seemed to love the idea of babies. I figured I was a baby too since I was with those other ones.

It had been a few days since I heard *Mummy loves you* voice, and I hadn't seen her yet. I noticed that when other babies cried, they would take them away and when they got back, they would be happy. So, this time I cried. I made sure I wasn't hungry, I didn't poo poo or tinkle. I wanted to see *Mummy loves you* voice. The nurses finally figured it out after an hour of me crying that I wanted to go to *Mummy loves you* voice.

We traveled out of the incubator room and down the halls. People kept stopping the nurse and they would say "AWEEE, she is so adorable!" I thought it was weird that they would talk about the nurse so often and always wanted to stop her. Didn't they know I had a meeting to go to? Apparently not because it kept going on, so I laid on the tears.

We finally made it to the room, and I made sure I had my big eyes open. I wanted to meet that soft voice who would sometimes invade my personal space. I needed an apology for not holding me yet and for the invasion of privacy. The nurse gave me to *Mummy loves you* voice and I forgot everything I needed to tell her. My memory wasn't quite good honestly as if memory was not a thing.

Mummy loves you voice said jokingly but seriously, "Nurse this is the wrong baby!" but I couldn't stop looking at her. She was so majestically beautiful. I wanted to play with her, I didn't care if I wasn't the baby she wanted at the moment. Not sure how this place works but maybe you can rent babies here. I knew she must have been on those drugs *Daddy's here* was talking about because she was the one I had been looking for. The nurse clarified my time and date of birth and confirmed I was the right baby! YAYYY! I get to stay. *Mummy loves you* voice said, "You have no color baby girl, but mommy loves you!" We spent hours together, I even fell asleep in her arms before the nurses took me back to the whole.

That bubble wasn't fun anymore and I felt like I was there for a very long time. One day *Daddy's here* voice held me tight and said comfortingly, "Little Red, Mommy and Daddy are going to finally take you home after months of being here, you're coming home!" Home, my bubbas and sissy blobs would always talk about home, they made it sound so cool. I couldn't wait to escape!

The doctors came in to reassure the exiting process and said I had to return for follow ups and more test, but I was free to go home. All the nurses I had met came to give out hugs. Nurse Gigi was my favorite, she was the first to call me Red when she noticed the color of the strands of hair I had on my head. I didn't have much compare to those other babies. I am actually not sure how she seen the strand because I didn't have any hair. She was the one nurse I was going to miss she always knew what I wanted and how I wanted it. We gave our farewells and we passed the infirmity. I saw my empty bubble and I was excited to leave!

Little Red was born on December 23, 1996 on a surprisingly warm winter day in Cleveland, OH. The first three years of her life, her and her family lived on 117th street near a neighborhood park on the west side of Cleveland. Her parents were separated at the age of three when her father went to prison and her mother moved back to Lorain, OH. At the age of eight, Red's father returned home and moved back in to their old house in Cleveland. She spent most of her summers with her Dad and the school year with her Mother. Co-parenting typically went smooth. Her father provided for Red as much as he could but her mother took a larger load of responsibility outside of finances. Where her parents could not support her, Gran stepped in to fill in the gaps.

Red was the youngest of four children with two brothers and the eldest being her sister. She has one uncle on her father's side and five on her mothers. One Aunt on her Dad's side through her Grandmothers marriage and four Aunts on her Mother's side. Growing up Red never considered herself to be anything outside of well off. She was highly spoiled and super grown. She spent a lot of time with her great grandmother when she was younger before she passed.

Great Gran, Queen Ester Riase, was legendary to Red. Red also had the privilege to be named after such a legend: Red Queenterah Riase. Sometimes they would call Red little queen. That wasn't often but it happened. Red could remember seeing Great Gran take on the world. She seemed like a super hero and she could handle everything. She would defend Red, adopt and raise kids in this huge home, prepare Sunday meals that were to die for and clean. She always made Red smile and Red didn't understand why one day she couldn't see Great Gran anymore.

She wasn't hurt but she did miss playing with Big Queen. Granny Gerrie was Great Gran's daughter and she did a good job filling in the gaps for Red. Red knew she had passed but it wasn't until Granny's visits to the cemetery that made it real. It was as if seeing Great Gran and not being able to hug or laugh with her anymore finally settle in once she said, "Hi, great gran" and got no reply.

I always wondered where Big Queen went, I knew she had passed but where do people go when they die? I was still fairly young and although my Granny explained that Big Queen was in heaven. I wanted to know where heaven was and how to go visit. I would ask questions upon questions trying to figure out if I could locate heaven. It was in the sky but where at in the sky? It was far away but could we drive there? How long would it take? Do you have to die to get there? Where is there?

My mind was bottled with questions and then my questions about God arose. Was he responsible for Big Queen leaving? Did he hurt her? How are we here? Who was the first person born? How did there get to be so many people from just two people? Why was life so confusing? Every time Gran answered a question, I had more questions about the answer. She used to tell me to relax my mind; it may not make sense, but it all adds up, which then confused me even more. If something doesn't make sense, then it can't add up. Of course, I was too young to explain that too her, so I took a nap instead.

Trying to figure out God, it's exhausting and way too much work. I really didn't question God much after Big Queen died, I was into figuring out people. It was much easier to analyze people and things I could see. I watched how my Dad and Mom argued, how my sister and brothers were all messed up. I looked up to my parents and siblings so I would watch them to figure how to act when I got older. Everything they did seemed legit until it felt weird.

I remember going over to a family members house and the adults were with the other adults and the kids were with the other kids. We played house, this is when I learned my first lesson on womanhood. We were never our ages when we played house. We were grown women and men playing house. We cooked, we cleaned, we played cards, we had kids, we humped, we were grown.

Red was about five when she discovered what the word "boyfriend" meant. When the adults were being adults and the kids stayed out their conversations, the kids were all in adult business. Red made transactions with her first boyfriend while playing seven minutes of heaven. It wasn't a huge transaction just a kiss, in a dark closet for seven minutes. Adult business is what Red knew.

Red's sister was always a tomb boy so Red was never comfortable with girls. She was always in boys faces and had multiple boyfriends. In the first grade, Red was okay with bubble invasion. She didn't know too much about sex beyond humping and kissing. Her mother was surprised as she began to spell S-E-X to her friend and Little Red said out loud "Sex, Mommy?"

There was this cute little boy named, Tony and every first-grade girl liked him. Red was one of them and he had the cutest fat cheeks. Cooddies were something Red was willing to accept from Tony. He would always sit by Red during story time and he had to pick with Red during gym. The gym teacher knew they liked each other and thought it was the cutest thing ever. The two were inseparable.

It was story time and Tony was really close to me. The teacher was reading when I felt something touch my back. It was Tony and I told him to stop before we got in trouble. He told me the teacher wasn't paying attention and I had seen adults do it before so I let his hand stay. Then he went further down my back closer to the peek of my butt and it sent chills down my spine. He went inside my panties and touch my buttocks, I didn't know what to do.

I had gotten use to guys always touching me but not like that. I wasn't comfortable but I did not say anything. I was too afraid of what people may say. Girls were called hoes in our school and because I didn't have many friends that were girls, I was one of them. So he kept doing it. It didn't go too far, but geese... I hated story time. I would try to go read to the Kindergarteners during our story time to avoid being touched. My teacher thought I was pretty smart and that I did well with younger children. Somehow the kids liked me, and I think they would ask for me. That was my way out and when I realized I wanted my bubble back.

Red was really strong willed, unless it came to herself. She would always defend others because she hated being taking advantage of. The problem was she fought everyone's battles except for her own. When she had turned eight, that's when her world turned upside down.

In the second grade, she noticed what a bully was, and it felt just as bad as anyone else who came in her world and took advantage of her. She would hold her composer if someone picked on her but as soon as someone picked on her friends, she spazzed. Red went to a school that taught Elementary to 12th grade students. While Red was still in the second grade, she encountered Rachel the 8th grader.

I was walking outside after the school bell rang and Mr. Bob let us leave. I noticed Rachel was talking to my friends. She had been picking on me for weeks now. She was yelling at my friends and I wanted to scream. Before I knew it, I was running over to Rachel and I pushed her into the street. She pushed me back but I wouldn't go down. I kept shooting my shots, dipping and diving.

My dad had came back home that year and we would practice boxing in the basement with his punching bag and gloves. He taught me about bobbing and weaving, using my body to control my punches and using my power arm to swing. He told me to only use these tools when necessary. I guess it became necessary because those short lessons came rushing in so quickly. I stood my ground and I got my hits in. I had one bruise, but Rachel had plenty.

The Principal must of broke it up and before I knew it I was in his office staring at the Five Principles to a successful student: 1. Listen 2. Learn 3. Be Kind… and "Red what were you thinking?", the Principal said. I honestly wanted to tell him the truth. I was thinking about how good it felt to whoop Rachel's tail. I had never been in the Principal's office for anything outside of good behavior… this was new. I kept my mouth shut because I wasn't sure if he really wanted my response.

He said he called my mom and instantly I began to cry. My brother went to school there too and my mom was always mad when he got in trouble. He would get whooping's and harsh punishments from my dad and mom. My life was once again over. I had come to the end of the road all because I made one bad turn. I just couldn't help it, it's like something came over me when I seen her making fun of my friends and I had to defend them.

I had to come up with a plan but my, oh my, I didn't know what to do. So I told the Principal the truth. My dad always said the truth would set you free. So I told him how she had been picking on me and my friends for a long time. I wanted to lie and say I was trying to calm her down before I attacked her but I couldn't, instead the truth came scrambling out. I realize I probably shouldn't have pushed her in the street considering all the cars but I couldn't help it.

When my mom got to the school, she was so mad at me in the Principal's office and I was terrified to get in the car. The Principal explained that he would talk to Rachel's family about bullying, but because I hit first, I did have to leave the school for a while. I knew that was going to be the loneliest ride home. My mom was disappointed and that hurt more than any yell or whooping could have. She sent me to my Dad's while I was out of school.

My Dad was upset that I was not in school, but it was more so because the Principal was a "No good punk who didn't realize my baby was doing what was right.", his words exactly. He asked me if I won and how many bruises did the girl have. I told him all my friends said I won and

Rachel was crying. For the first time, I seen what I did may have been wrong to others but it was right to my Dad, me and my friends.

Red was never the same after that conversation with her dad but she stopped letting people bully her. She stood up for herself and sometimes she was a bit cocky. As long as she could fight back, she wasn't going to allow anyone else to treat her like crap.

THE TRIGGER

Confidence can go a long way in a young woman's life. It's the difference from accepting anything to accepting what's right. It can also be the difference from hate and love. Defending others made Red feel like some kind of superhero and took her away from feeling so weak all the time. She had handled the bullying and the confidence until that summer.

I had gotten my first girl best friend when I turned eight. My best friend's mom was Mom's best friend too, I think. They worked together, they hung out and they trusted each other. Seemed like a best friend kind of thing. Me and my best friend went to the same school. We shared everything, and the teacher had a hard time separating us. I used to love going over to her house. She had an older brother who was about four years older than us. He was a boy and it was my natural instinct to think they wanted something from me.

The first couple of times I came over I wouldn't really notice him, he would pick on us, but he wouldn't stay in the room long. He seemed like my brothers just a weirdo boy. My girl best friend played house differently than the other kids I knew. We wouldn't do the adult business games, but we would talk like adults and cuss at our barbies.

I think her brother was old enough to watch us and when mommy and her best friend had to work together, he would. He came in the room and he asked what we were playing. She told him to leave we were playing house. Then he would ask to play. I hated when boys got involved, they ruined everything. I told her to tell him no, but bestie said it would be fun. He played a little differently than the other kids too. There wasn't any humping but there was a lot of touching. He moved our hands on the middle section of his pants and I felt something rising. It was weird and uncomfortable.

I had gotten tired of house it was only kind of normal in school, not even sure what normal means anymore. Mom had to drop me off to go to work and for the longest, that was the only place I could go to. This time I didn't want to go over my best friend's house. My aunts said I was a cry baby and they refused to keep me, so that wasn't an option. Geese, I really wish I would have been sweeter to them. I asked if I could go with Mom but it was Friday and I never went with Mom on weekends. She worked at the bar and sometimes I was allowed to go for a little bit. The owner, Richie, was so nice to our family ; he would give me free chips and fountain drinks from this long spray hose thingy.

My Mom was in a rush and she couldn't see the fear in my eyes. Granted I never told her about anything. I figured I had to be like mommy and daddy. I could hear them crying or arguing and they never told me anything. I slept with mommy a lot and I can remember waking up in the middle of the night to her crying underneath the blanket. I didn't even know what to call what happened to me. So I figured I would go in and act like I wasn't feeling good. Seen my mom do it all the time when she didn't want to go to work and it seemed to work.

I did play for a little bit until he came home from school. He stayed at school a little longer than us and I used that to my advantage. When he got home, I asked if we could just watch TV because I wasn't feeling good. He didn't bother us and I thought I could relax. Then his mom stepped out to grab some dinner. That's when he told me to come to his room. I didn't want to play house anymore so I just sat there and his sister kept telling me her brother wanted me.

If she was anything like me and my brothers, I don't blame her for not realizing how much I did not want to go. She kept telling me he just wants to play and they do it all the time. I knew older people always knew more about life than I did but I didn't like this part of life. After he said please, that he wasn't going to play house, he just needed to ask me a question I mustered the strength to go to his room and slammed the door open.

He told me to sit on the floor and went toward the door to shut it. This wasn't like the Principal's office; I was terrified more so because I didn't know what was going on. He sat on the bed and asked if I had ever seen a penis. I had seen them when my brothers would run around the house naked but I didn't tell him that. I never know when adults want your real response. So I didn't say anything. He told me to get closer to him and I didn't want to. This was definitely not house.

When I didn't move he grabbed my arm and squeezed my arm until tears slowly fell on my face. I was trying to be an adult and hold it all together. I told him I was sorry and I would play house. He yelled at me and told me shut up. I was so terrified because I knew you were supposed to listen to adults but in that moment I didn't understand why. Then he pulled me closer and pulled down his pants.

It looked so disgusting and it stood straight up. He grabbed my arm again and told me if I scream, he would kill me. I remembered the end of the world feeling and I didn't want life to be over. I just wanted my mommy. So I didn't scream. He pushed my face in toward his penis and told me to open my mouth. It went in and out, out and in for what seemed like forever. I tried to push away. I felt like I was going to gag but he pushed harder and faster. He yanked my head back and told me to say "Papi." I held in my tears and I started trembling.

I guess I didn't say it fast enough so he smacked my butt. He pushed me to the ground and told me to pull down my pants. I had never seen a monster until that moment. I could see in his eyes he was enjoying torturing me. I still couldn't understand why I was supposed to listen to adults. He pulled down my flowered Friday panties, laid on me and then his sister busted in the room.

She said mommy was coming and asked me if I was okay and I tried to run to the bathroom before he grabbed my arm again. He told me that if I ever said anything about what happened he would hurt my family. I had never been that scared in my life and I wanted to go home. I pulled my clothes up in shame and ran to the bathroom with my head down. After I sat near the toilet and threw up, I asked mommy's best friend if I could call my mom and she told me that my mom was at work and I had to wait till she got off. I wanted to cry and yell but I couldn't formulate words to explain anything, all I had was tears. That's when her son came down stairs and said he was going to his friends.

She told him to call her when he got there. He gave her a hug and walked out the room. I never got robbed before but I feel like he took something that didn't belong to him. I stumped my way back up the stairs and tried to play with his sister. She kept asking if I was okay and if I had fun. I had so many questions about what fun was to her but I did not want to know the answers so I took a nap hoping that when I woke up my mom would be there.

I woke up three times before I realized I couldn't sleep and I stayed under the cover with my eyes wide open. My mind tried to understand how she thought that was fun, why was fun so terrifying and how I don't want to have fun ever again. I kept replaying that moment in my head and finally I heard my Mom's voice. I think I almost fell down the stairs and left some school work there trying to get out. Mommy's best friend told her that I wasn't feeling well and she could tell because I was being bratty that day. She assumed that I was being bad because I didn't feel well. I almost wish I didn't play sick.

We got in the car and I sat in the back seat when the tears just started flowing. I couldn't murmur any noise so mommy didn't know I was crying on the way back home. She parked the car, got her stuff out the trunk and told me to unbuckle my seat. I wiped my tears and I got out the car to help mommy with her stuff. After we got in the house, I dropped the bags and ran straight into my room, got under my covers and went to sleep.

Mommy must have been putting things away because she took a minute to come check on me. She turned the lights on and asked if I was okay. I was still confused so I pretended to be sleep. She turned the lights back off after my sister complained that she was tired. The morning came and everybody left to their friends houses.

Mommy asked if I wanted to go get my best friend for ice cream and I broke the code. I spilled out my problems knowing that is not what adults do. I yelled at mommy, I told her I never want to play house again. Mommy didn't understand and she asked me, "why not?" As much as I wanted to tell the full truth I couldn't I was so afraid of what he might do. So I protected his sister. I told mommy that he would make us touch him with his clothes on and when I wasn't there, he would make his sister touch him without clothes on. Somehow being a superhero felt better when I was protecting others.

After Red finished her superhero duties, things got pretty ugly. Red felt like she had done more destruction than good. This time telling the truth turned everything upside down. She didn't realize that her or her mom would lose their best friends . She wasn't aware of what a court room looked like until she told the truth. Red's father was extremely upset with Red's mom, the whole family felt split like Moses at the Red Sea and Red thought it was all her fault. They switched school systems and Red didn't see her best friend for a very long time.

Red hated moving, they had moved so many times and packing was not fun. It turned out to be a good decision for Red though mainly because, she didn't know too many people at her new school so she could start over. She excelled in school and even skipped a grade. She went straight from second to fourth grade and she passed with flying colors.

Unfortunately, at the time the state law had not passed the decision to continue, Red in advanced classes, so she had to take fourth grade over. Before she knew it, it was time to move again to another school system and new friends.

Red's brothers had lots of friends and some were even considered her family. One friend, Jordan, was truly one of her brothers. He was always over and seemed to never leave. He would defend Red when her other brothers and sister would ridicule her. She loved when Jordan was over. It was them against the world. Everyone thought Jordan was a part of the family and no one could say differently. Jordan's mom thought that the family had adopted him that year because his mom hardly ever seen him.

I didn't have many friends at that time. I was glued to my mommy. I was afraid for bad things to happened and it seemed easier to just be with her. I would make mud pies by myself and my friends were worms and ants. I would try to play with my siblings, but no one actually liked to play with me outside of Jordan. Angelo probably liked me the most out of my real siblings but Jordan was like the brother I wish I had.

There were two rooms and an attic in our house for sleeping. My sister, Marie had her own room, I slept with my mommy and my brothers slept in the attic. Jordan stayed up their too. I really did think he was my brother. It was weird though he came out of nowhere, he wasn't like my other brothers because they had been around much longer. Everyone was comfortable with Jordan because he was family.

I would play with Jordan alone sometimes, we loved playing with my Barbies and my brothers' action figures. We would go places in our mind, to the moon, to the beach and many more places that seemed so real. Our imaginary adventures where the best. Jordan would read me stories when my mom came home late and I couldn't sleep. He would bring me ice-cream back from the ice-cream store down the street or just candy from the candy man. No one could tell me anything bad about Jordan.

We were all playing cops and robbers and then my older brother, Biggs, he went to take out the trash. My eldest brother, Angelo, was at practice so it was just me and Jordan for a little. I was playing with my Barbies and he was telling me about this time his dad touched him. I felt bad for him, but I didn't tell him what happened to me. I was still playing with my Barbies and he said he wanted to show me what his dad did. I honestly didn't think he had to show me, and I thought I heard my brother coming up the stairs. Instead he asked if we wanted anything from the store because he was going down the street.

I wanted some chocolate candy, so I yelled down the stairs and asked for chocolate. Jordan went in his book bag and got some money and said to bring back three chocolate bars. My sister was down stairs and my mom was at work.

It was normal to leave me with Jordan because he was so sweet. He even offered to get me more chocolate.

I went back to playing with my Barbies, they were in the running to become the first woman president. Jordan pretended to listen to my electoral speech and he would clap when I was finished. I wanted to go down stairs to get my Barbies brush because her hair was looking crazy. That's when Jordan told me to raise my hands, then he picked me up and swirled me in the air. I loved rides with Jordan. We fell on the bed and he sat me on his lap while he lied down.

Jordan didn't do that normally and I just thought we fell. He was moving up and down and he told me to play cow girl. He was the horse and I was the cowgirl. It was weird because I had this feeling that I never felt before. It was a tingly pulse in my kitty Kay (that's what mama called it after the case with our old best friends), and I didn't know what to do with it. It got worse every time he went up and down. He didn't make me feel bad because I knew he would never hurt me. I never questioned him when he wanted to play that game. I thought it was weird that we only played when we were by ourselves. I asked him once if we could play when my brothers were around, and he put me on his back. I actually preferred that method better because I didn't have that tingly feeling.

I never told my family about those cow girl moments because I thought Jordan was family so I must have been overreacting . I assumed that's how men protected you because he made me feel safe. I didn't know that it was going to affect me in the same way that my best friend's brother did. Jordan never did leave the family, but it was time for the family to move again. I packed up my bags and tried to make sense of my life.

Red didn't really like making new friends because she always had to get rid of them. Her mom had gotten a new best friend and she had a daughter named, Elly. Elly and Red were forced to get to know each other but this time there was not a brother. Red and Elly got into a lot of trouble together before the move. One time Red gave Elly some of her asthma pills and got Elly really sick. Those pills made Red feel like a fresh tank of air was given to her. She had taken them most of her life because the doctors were afraid she might not make the next asthma attack. She figured the pills were magical and thought they would help Elly. Red was in so much trouble, but they were still kids.

Elly had moved across the street from Red's new school and that was Red's new location. She still wasn't a household favorite from her Aunts and Uncles so she had to grow close to Elly. She just wished she didn't have to bring someone else into her scrambled mind. Especially when none of her issues seemed to be addressed within the family and not being able to talk to anyone outside the family. Red's emotions were limited to a certain box but she couldn't get into the box to let them out.

There was a rule in her house. What happens in this house stays in this house. What happens in this family stays in this family. There was no talking about things Red didn't understand unless it was with family. Even within family it had to be cleared by Red's mom or dad. Neither side of the family would know what was going on in what house. The only thing that was clear is that Red had no outlet to understand what was going on.

Red's sexual desires had grown so much in two years that she was an adventurous kid. Her and Elly would play house and hump with panties on when Elly's mom was sleep or just running errands. Red and Elly would watch sex stuff on TV or play highly sexual R&B and Hip Hop music when no one was paying attention to them. Somehow they knew what the goodies were that Cierra was saying no to. They understood how "bootylicious", Beyoncé said they were. Sir mix a lot taught them how to do the humpty hump and do it baby.

They became two peas and a pie. They were very close and defended each other all the time. The summer before school started, they played at the school park and Elly's boy neighbor, Tucker, came to play with them. Tucker was very strange but he was in the neighborhood.

More boys came and more girls came to the park. The boys were with boys playing basketball and the girls at the playground. Tucker started teasing the girls and throwing mulch. Apparently he didn't understand that you don't

change up on the people you came with. Red had enough
of boys being rude and she threw mulch back. They got in
each other's faces and were yelling and then the boy pushed
Red. Red never did stop her lessons with her dad and she
just started using her strong hand to swing, bob and weave.

Tucker was beat up black and blue before he ran back
home to tell his dad. Red got in serious trouble that day
when his dad threatened to call the police. Elly's mom
must have convinced him not to and Red and Elly had to
apologize. They never seen him after that moment. Red was
grounded for a week straight until school started.

My dad, Leo, never whooped me but my mom, Charly,
would. Whenever I got into a fight my dad always made
sure my intentions were good and then he would tell me
stories about when he was younger. My dad wasn't tall
but he was a fighter. He told me how one time he stood
on the lunchroom table to beat some kid up. My dad was
legendary to me. He would also tell me the consequences
of his actions and remind me that people really aren't worth
my time. I always wondered what happened to my dad for
those five years he was missing. I knew he was in prison but
what did he do? I didn't learn that lesson until I was much
older.

My momma was a fighter too, but I didn't learn that
until she got in momma-defense mode. Momma defense
mode is a symptom that occurs when momma's babies
are being threatened. One day, the teacher was mad at my

brother Biggs and I guess there wasn't a logical decision made for his punishment. And in the heat of the moment , my mom revealed herself. I thought wow, I have both my legendary dad and my secret weapon momma. She told us how she fought my brother's teacher back when they were in high school and the teacher was just mad.

Red's family dynamic is something near strange. She dealt with molestation from family and friends of family, suffered depression from bullies and boiled anger for men by the age of 10 years old. These consequences ultimately led to a trigger that once pulled had destroyed a once innocent life. A life that grew up for the next couple of years trying to figure out what was wrong with it. A life that felt it was born with a defect and needed a recall. She will never be able to undue the things that happened to her but she can learn from them.

I have a saying that I live by that says, "My past doesn't own me, it owes me." — Mo Speaks (Really cool speaker I met along the way). I remember when I started living by this, it was much later in my life but God is the main reason I was able to come to that conclusion. I would like to interrupt your reading to remind you that you hold so much value in this world. That what happened to you in your past, is going to be your biggest blessing. Stay focused on God and he will bring clarity and rewards you didn't think you were capable of receiving.

Don't allow your past to put you into shame because we all go through things. We have our own way of dealing with pain, hurt and trauma. There is no perfect way to heal and each of us are finding out what works for us. I do not blame any of the men who touched me. I do not blame myself. I have to come to the conclusion that God needed me to experience what I experience to tear the mold of incest, molestation and rape that runs rapid in our generational bloodlines.

THE REACTION

Imagine it is Halloween and you have a bag of candy full of your favorite and least favorite sweets. My favorite candy bar is a Babe Ruth, my Papa Flence introduced it to me. My least favorite candy is the Milky Way that was first introduced in the white neighborhood I went to. We all have favorite and least favorite preferences when it comes to candy, food, clothes, etc. Do you remember who introduced you to your preferences? Are you like me where you avoid the least favorites and go searching for the favorites until you eat it all up? Do you throw the candy away that you don't like or give it away? I always kept the Babe Ruths because they remind me of my Papa. I had known Papa Flence since I was a baby and he was so caring. He never did anything to hurt me, he spoiled me beyond a shadow of a doubt and he showed me one of the first examples of love. I was always under him and we were kind of inseparable when I was younger. He's the real MVP, I just wish I would have remembered the love he and my father showed when I encountered other men.

Granted I was young, but once I was introduced to sexual intimacy it was like a Milky Way chocolate bar. I tried to avoid it, I tried to eat up everything else that was good in my life but at the end of the day, it was still in my bag. Didn't matter if I threw my feeling away or not, it was like it had an anniversary date and it would come back to weigh me down. I couldn't give it away because I didn't want anyone else to have to suffer with such a unpleasant taste. Sometimes I would leave it in the little room in my head called DO NOT DISTURB! That would only cause it to be stale and take up space for my growth. When do you get tired of carrying a load of unwanted sweets and give it to someone who is able to handle it?

Red was twelve carrying around a full bag of Milky Ways and she didn't know what the heck to do with them. She knew, most men, if not all, gave out the Milky Ways and started looking for ways to carry more because she figured they would have more to give her regardless. She would create storage bins for these unwanted feelings and emotions. One day her Milky Ways fell out the bag and there was no more room in the storage bins. She ran out of options and she didn't know how to handle her feelings.

She had to watch two children while their parents went to work. As she changed one of the baby boys, her mind flooded with thoughts about touching this cute, precious little baby in a way she had been touched in her past. She felt so disgusting and thought how could she dare do anything to an innocent baby.

I fought the feelings, I didn't want to do anything that could harm that baby. I didn't know whether to pray or just put the baby in the crib and walk away. I chose to walk away and talk to a boy that was my age on the phone. Praying was still an uncertain thing for me, I knew you did it at night before going to bed but not when your thoughts were trying to overthrow you. Talking to that boy felt less wrong then thinking about harming the baby. Me and that boy had planned on seeing each other the next day to chill at his house. I knew what that meant but I hadn't lost my virginity yet. I thought maybe I wanted it this time since I was thinking about it so much.

I didn't think I was pretty at that time, I didn't have boobs yet like my classmates and my freckles were weird. I remember trying to scrub my face off once to get rid of them, but it wasn't working. I was tired of being a giraffe or broken chocolate chip cookie. I had gotten over my emotion to seduce a baby, but for some reason I wanted to see if that cute little face reacted to my boobs. So, I flashed my boobs out really quickly, like my momma was going to barge in the door, it felt weird and maybe inappropriate to even have them out. Adults got dressed in front of kids all the time I figured this was better than my other thoughts. I couldn't do it like the lifetime movies the kids mother would watch with me if I ever just came over to visit. Where the baby sitter would make the kids fall in love with her and do bad stuff. She ended up going crazy or in jail anyway, so I avoided that kind of babysitting. I didn't know what jail looked like, but that court house was pretty scary.

He kind of just looked at me like it was a game of peek-a-boo and started giving baby laughs. He was cracking up and I knew he was just a baby, but I felt ridiculed. What was I thinking? If a baby looks at me like this there's no way, I am taking my shirt off for intimacy with that boy! That was the last time I ever did that again. I was too ashamed, and it literally took me forever to be comfortable in my skin. I wish I could go back and apologize to that little boy, he may not remember but if he does, he could have a perception about women that were as negative as my perception of men was. Little boy and all the other little boys who may have experience something like that from a woman, I would like to apologize on our behalf. I didn't mean to do it, I feel really bad, I hope you can forgive me. I am not making excuses for myself but it made me think differently about why boys did what they did to me.

I didn't loose my virginity the next day, for some reason my fear would creep in because I didn't want to feel like I was less than. I was afraid of what my mom might say, I was afraid of what boys would do to me. I was afraid that I would be the reason for everything that happened to me if I just accepted the thoughts in my head. Those thoughts were so loud and violent. Those thoughts convinced me that I was sexy at the age of 12 and that every man wanted one thing. Those thoughts made me afraid to hug men to a point I couldn't show my own dad affection. Those thoughts interrupted every relationship I had until I sat down and dealt with my bag of Milky Ways.

I had been taken advantage of for what seemed like forever only problem was I wasn't always aware. When I tried to run past my thoughts, I would be kicked back into that room where I tried to hide them. My cousins, not all of them but a few, were equally worse than any other men I had ever met. They were the first ones to touch me intimately, with more than one finger inside of me. Every time I wanted to trust men, men showed me who men were. I had gotten to a point where I became a loner. I could finally stay home on my own and I took that route every time. I had plenty of books to keep me busy and I could socialize at school.

Red's family thought something was wrong with her, she never wanted to go over friends houses and she preferred to read a book on Friday nights. It didn't help that her own family laughed at her for trying to stay away from fears. No one asked why she always reading a book without saying she was a lame or introvert. People made conclusions about who Red was and she really just wanted to figure that out herself. She liked being alone though it gave her time to look up porn. She figured out a way to please herself without men being involved. She never watched porn with men in it was always lesbian sex. Something about penises through Red off. She would imitate what those girls did to themselves and even had crazy sex dreams that felt entirely too real. You don't even want to know what happened to Mr. Bear.

Although she appreciated her alone time, she responded well with other kids, but it was like pulling teeth trying to get her to be a child and enjoy the world. Maybe she felt like she was already grown and had a hard time relating. Most kids at that time were spending the night over friends' homes, dating, having normal fun. Red didn't think the world had much to offer but those books took her mind places. She had gone back to being bullied in school because she didn't act like the other kids. She still tried to fit in so she could at least enjoy school. She wasn't being a hero because she was too busy trying to laugh the pain away.

By the end of the school year Red had found love with someone who actually noticed her. His name was Ru, and he was two year older and stopped her dead in her tracks to get her number. Ru wasn't that much taller than Red and there were a lot of girls who wanted Ru. He was pretty popular and knew just about everybody. Red had never notice him until that last day of sixth grade year.

I just loved the last day of the school year, I got to wear a white shirt my mom didn't care about, and everyone wrote on my shirt in permanent marker. I wrote on everyone else's too, I always wrote things to make people smile, like a fun memory or just something special I noticed about them. I loved reading my shirt sometime during the summer it made me smile. There was this older boy named, Ru who came into my classroom to visit the teacher. I hadn't noticed him that whole year, he was kind a cute but I kept my distance. I had books and now a new shirt to read, I tried to stray away from boys I didn't know.

Someone was signing the front of my shirt when I felt a marker near the lower section of my back. I turned around and it was, RU! AHHHHHHH!! this was not happening to me. Like he actually noticed me, and I didn't do anything. While he was writing, I kept thinking about how exciting it was going to be to read whatever he said. I turned to look at him and he gave me a hug. Oh My, the butterflies that went up my spine. It was love at first hug before I even knew what that meant. He asked me for my number, and I gave it to him. I had to explain to him that I could only text during the day but we could make calls any time after 9 p.m. because of my Dad's phone plan.

Ru was my summer boo, and we pillow talked like every night until like 5 a.m. I learned how to dirty text with Ru, it wasn't hard because I had already had these grown thoughts in my head from the last 12 or so years of my life. I sent sexy photos to him and deleted them out of my phone ASAP. I felt like my dad could see my photos if he wanted considering we had Verizon and maybe they could show him my gallery. They weren't too bad I had all my clothes on, but they were some sexy poses, boob lifts, booty-poken grown photos.

I wanted to visit him one time, but I knew my mom wouldn't just let me go over a boy's house. I needed an exit plan, and then I met my best friend, Taylee. People at school picked on her worse than they picked on me, but I met her during one of our bus routes ; she lived down the street from me. Taylee was actually pretty dope and she didn't really get into trouble until the summer we met. My mom always thought she was a bad influence on me but honestly, I think it was the opposite. Ru had told us to meet him at a party, my mom was okay with the party mainly because it was at my cousin's house.

I got dressed at Taylee's house, nothing too shameful but I had short shorts (with my big ole thighs) and a long sleeve shirt. If your wondering why on earth I had on a long sleeve that's another story for another time. We went to the party and had a blast, I think I established street cred that day and found out my cousin Rosie was coming to my middle school next year. I think I might have that advantage for my life.

I was sitting on Ru's lap and, him and Taylee became best friends. I was okay with that for about 2 minutes and told Taylee she needed to find her own boo so I can become best friends with him. Not even minutes later, this big head boy, with this cool-aid smile came stumbling down the stairs. I thought to myself, Taylee and him would be perfect for each other. I was really just trying to not have Ru and Taylee so close.

It didn't work that way though, she did end up liking Mr. Cool-aid, and he did become her best friend, but her and Ru were still tighter than ever. That was by far the greatest summer I had ever experienced. I went to parties, I was with RU almost every day but mom thought I was with Taylee. Taylee was with us too though and DeAndre (Mr. Coolaid) he was hilarious, best decision I ever made for someone else. Dre was really my best friend I had never had a best friend like him before. He was funny, smart, he listened, and tried to make since of my boy problems. He was always getting in trouble though, so I didn't really get see him often but when we caught up it was like time wasn't a thing that passed us by.

Me and Ru had a relationship that summer and I didn't do anything I didn't want to do. Including sex, I did everything but sex. Something about having sex through me off. It put me in a state of fear so I would try to ease my way out whenever things got really hot. When it was time for school to start back up Ru and I started walking home together. I was pretty far from school, but Ru was like a 10-minute walk away. I had been proving myself as a tease all summer and I think Ru was getting tired of it. We were walking when his cousin, German, had caught up with us one day.

I never noticed German but he told me to call him Manny. He was pretty cool, a lot taller than Ru and they lived down the street from each other. Ru seemed a little off that day but German carried a pretty good conversation. He asked how old I was, of course I was the youngest, and he was trying to figure out why I didn't know who he was. I was trying to discover the same thing because I don't remember seeing him. He started becoming me and Ru's walking body.

The next day at school, Ru had some older girl come up to me during lunch and tell me that he was breaking up with me. Can you believe the nerve of that little boy? I acted like it didn't mean anything because I had an image to maintain, but deep inside, I wanted to blow up. Why send someone? Why not be a man? I knew other girls were happy because they couldn't understand why he like me anyway. I didn't understand it either, but I was not about to break down in tears in front of those people. I shrugged it off and continued my conversation with someone else like nothing happened. Literally said okay, did you finish your homework girl?

I was getting ready to get on the bus that day because there was no way I was about to walk home alone then Taylee convinced me to walk. I didn't see Ru on the way home and we walked our normal walk even passed his house. Before we got to his house, I did see German and he said if I ever needed to talk, I should call him. He gave me his number I explained the same 9 p.m. drill to him. I didn't text him but somehow I think Taylee must have given him my number. We started texting and he was everything I needed. I was trying to figure out why his cousin was being weird. Ru literally just dropped off the face of Earth, no text all school year.

It was more like a friendship than anything else. I knew about his girl problems and he listened to issues I had with his cousin. I thought nothing else of it until one day when Manny and I were walking home. Taylee had been home sick that day. Manny asked if I wanted something to drink because he wanted to walk me home he just needed to stop at his house. I said yes but more so because Manny had a dog and I loved dogs. I was a sucker for pets. So happy Manny was not a serial killer or anything because that's what they do, lure you in with pets or candy and kidnap you. I walked in the house, sat down as he put his stuff up. I even met his mother for a brief 10 minutes of my life before she left for work.

His mom was hilarious, I heard her over the phone a few nights while we were talking. She just knew my name not my face. Before she left, she told us, "Don't do nothing that I might have to whoop yo a** for later and little girl don't have no babies." We both kind of laughed, I didn't even think about Manny like that. Manny gave me something to drink and he told me I really don't deserve to be treated the way his cousin did me. Manny thought I was smart, and I could have any boy I wanted honestly. I didn't see myself that way but he said it was the way I carried myself. I wasn't falling over boys or trying to get their attention all the time. I still didn't see how any of this mattered.

He asked if I wanted to stay for a little bit and I didn't care. I had my homework with me so I just finished that. He had went to his room to play his game and I walked back there after I finished my homework. I tried to act like I knew what I was doing because I had NBA 2K11 on my WII but it was much different on his Xbox. He pulled me onto his lap and helped me navigate the controller. HOW did I let him get me like this? I know I was thinking that too. Then he started touching on my booty and ooh child it felt so good. Yes, I am still like 13 at the time but my body had urges that I couldn't always explain. Between that bed, those kisses and the game we lost, I don't think I even thought about what I was doing.

Manny got me good, we didn't have sex but my, oh my I wanted to. My mom kept calling my phone and I knew I had to go. So, I asked him to walk me home because it was getting dark. It wasn't until I got home that I realized how horrible I was to do that to Ru. Even though Ru had disappeared from my life I still felt weird because that was his cousin. I was trying to avoid Manny but it wasn't working. We walked home more, I stopped by more, my mom called more. One day I told Manny we needed to tell Ru and at first Manny didn't see why but I just felt bad.

THE CYCLE

Everyone went to late skate on Friday nights and Red knew Ru was going to be there, so she told Manny that they should tell him Friday. You can only imagine how that went down. Imagine your 13 year-old self being faced with a decision to tell your ex your dating his cousin. Imagine the rumors and the name calling she was about to endure. Red didn't even think about that when she came up with this grand master plan. She just didn't want to feel bad anymore. Leo, (Red's Dad) always said the truth will set you free.

Manny and Red had a lot of people on their side surprisingly who pushed them to go for it. When they broke the news to Ru, he kind of shrugged it off and said he didn't care. Red couldn't tell that he did what she did when the older girl broke the news to her, but she didn't care. She felt better and he hadn't talked to her in months so he must have been okay with it. But after that late skate, it's like Ru had a sudden interest in Red again. He started walking with Taylee again, who would walk with Manny and Red.

Ru would try to kiss Red and honestly Manny and Ru had some twisted idea about who owned Red. Then Ru would flirt with Taylee it was just a bunch of twisted middle school drama. Red didn't realize what she was allowing to happen, how it was affecting a family relationship and her morals. When her and Manny broke up they were still really close friends but DeAndre hated them together.

My best friend was really upset when I told him I was dating Manny; I never knew why either. He would tell me not to date him because he was only in it for one reason. The only problem was me and Manny still never did anything. Me and Manny never officially broke up; we just knew we were done, and Dre wanted me to stay away. I tried to listen to Dre, but Manny always found his way back in my life.

We did take a break and I would date other boys. I had a boyfriend in 7th grade and I would babysit across the street from his house. That was my favorite house to baby sit at for the longest. I just loved Jay's babies. Jay had two kids with Jackson, and they were like my own nieces and nephews. I adored Jay's babies and would do anything to watch them. Regardless if my boyfriend lived across the street or not.

Jay was normally at work when I would baby sit but I use to come over after school too and just eat all her food, play with the kids, and visit my boyfriend. I came over to watch the kids and their cousin while Jay was at work and Jackson was down the street with his business partners. I put the kids to sleep and laid down in the youngest room because he would wake up more often than the girls. I was sleep for all of 15 minutes when I heard someone come up the stairs. It was just Jackson, so I closed my eyes to go back to sleep. He was in the bathroom, so I didn't have to protect the babies from robbers.

I opened my eyes for a moment when I saw the bathroom light. He checked on the girls and then he came to check on his son. He turned the lights on, stepped over me and went by his sons' bed. I think he gave him a kiss. I was still pretending to be sleep because I didn't really know Jackson so there was no conversation to hold. Then he turned the lights off and I knew he was leaving so I closed both of my eyes. I still felt like Jackson was in the room and I figured he was being a weird dad gazing at his children. He seemed to really care about his babies the way that Jay did.

Then he walked near me, and I thought he was going to ask if I was okay. Instead he came to lay by me, I could tell he was drunk, so I thought maybe he just wanted to go to bed. So, I tried to clutch my eyes tighter, so I wouldn't speak to him and then I felt his hand on my butt. He just rubbed me for hours, he put his hands inside my panties, and he told me I was beautiful. Then he got on top of me and pressed his self on my butt, he kept pressing, and pressing until he told me to roll over. I didn't want to lose my virginity like this. I could feel tears coming but I had to hold them in. So, I acted like I couldn't hear him hoping someone would come in the room but even better the baby woke up.

He kind of fell off of me, not sure if it was shock, fear or God (maybe He pushed him off) but either way I have never been more excited to hear a baby cry, I got up and said I need to get the baby. I held the baby for hours trying to put him back to sleep. Jackson finally went back down stairs and I cried for like 30 minutes with that baby in my hand. I put the baby down when I heard Jay come in the door a few hours later and I tried to go back to sleep.

Sleep had been impossible with my mind racing about where Jackson was so I called Manny. I didn't call my boyfriend because I had never had a deep conversation or cried with him. He was just something to have in that moment for me but Manny knew me and he could handle this. Manny knew I had experienced this so many times, so he calmed me down and threaten to kill Jackson. He stayed on the phone with me until my mom came and got me.

I didn't tell my mom because I didn't want to hurt her feelings and I still kind of wanted to baby sit Jay's babies. I didn't go over there as often as I normally would, and my boyfriend wanted to see me, but I didn't want to be there. I would try to see him every once and while, but it was over for us really. When we broke up, I was fine, my friends thought I played him for Manny which may be true, but I also couldn't manage to go over there. Jackson would text me grown up things that I wasn't ready to do, and I couldn't continue the cycle.

That cycle wanted to follow me everywhere I went, and I just needed to avoid it in that moment. It seemed like as one cycle paused another began and I was exhausted. Me and Manny started dating again after the whole incident at Jay's but this time I wanted to keep him. We would kiss in the halls during lunch or after school ended. I had many annoying teachers, but the bald man was a hater. He snitched on me to the principle and then they told my mom all about the one kiss he seen me give Manny. Thank God he only seen the one kiss.

That was the most embarrassing parent teacher meeting ever. My mom stopped coming to schools after my 4th grade year because my teachers never had anything negative to say and my grades were excellent. This was one of the first times she really meant any of my academic leaders in a long time and it was all bad news. I could tell she was disappointed and then she requested to see Manny. I feel like there should have been laws against students stating their case without legal guardianship.

It is a horrible feeling to know that your mother who expects greatness from you is disappointed in you. That's where it hurt the most and when the tears began to roll out. When she requested to see Manny, I felt so insecure. My siblings use to tell me that I was ugly when I cried, and Manny had never seen me like that. He had heard me crying but never seen me. When he walked in that room, my tears where wiped faster than sonic chasing after coins. My mom made Manny promise to be done with me and I knew my life was over. How dare her dictate my breakups without even considering the damage it could do.

Manny was terrified of Charly and he stuck to his word. He avoided Red for a while and when conversations started back up, he strayed away from anything intimate. By 8th grade year, Manny and Ru went off to the high school and Red only see them after school. Red had become highly rebellious after her encounter with the Principal, the bald man teacher and her mom. There was this group her cousin Rosie had started in the 7th grade that Red joined called ~&Pretty and by 8th grade, this group ran the school.

This gave Red street credit and power. Red probably didn't know how to handle that kind of power at the time because to avoid losing it she belittled those who had no chance. ~&Pretty was an all-girl group who could make you or break you in middle school. Most people avoided their judgment but stayed on their good side. ~&Pretty also had access to all the cute boys, it's almost like people had to get approval on who to date through this group. Red could not afford not to mold into power.

This group made headlines; all teachers, principals and security guards knew who they were. Red was the mother or calm one out of the group of eight because she seemed so wise. She also became a bully to protect her spot often. They called her the Jokkar, but she wasn't really funny in comedy battles: it was more so that she knew how to make you laugh. Matter fact she hated comedy battles because she didn't have quick jokes, she had to think a little longer in battles. She tried to stand up for people but often times that threatened her safety.

Rosie threw all of the parties, knew where the next move was and had all the inside news. Vonka was the trouble maker and probably the funniest in the group. Mandy was an instigator, but she was really pretty. Nasia was the hype man, she knew how to dance, fight, laugh, and be loud. Danna was the auntie, she made sure they didn't get too out of line, but she acted a fool with them too. Emma was the sweet one who they so desperately needed. Kristie was the quite one, but she completed the group. These girls made Red's day, they kept her laughing and gave her reason to move through her nightmare life.

No one in the group was perfect, everyone had their own flaws, but they became family. They may not have been the best family, they did some serious dirt to people, but they were a family. A family that Red had not experienced in such a long time. It might have brung out the worse of Red but they also brung Red something vibrant, happiness.

Since Manny was forced out of the picture, Ru and Red got closer. I know your thinking what the heck is wrong with Red. She didn't know either. Ru made huge strides to get Red back. He started visiting Red's home when Charly (Red's Momma) wasn't around. Red would also visit Ru when his parents weren't home either. All of Red's other friends had already lost their virginity by this time and Red thought it was time for her to lose hers.

She would tell her friends that she was raped when she was younger, so she technically already lost her virginity, so they didn't think she was a goody tooshu. In reality Red was never penetrated with someone's man part, although there were many unwanted inserts. She may have been sexually assaulted many times, but she hadn't had sex yet. There was always an interruption before the piercing of her walls with another mans penis. They say that God blocks things maybe he was protecting her. Ru seemed to be into Red this time seriously and Manny was kicked out forever so she would get intimate to Ru.

Today was the day I lose virginity. Me and Ru had been texting pretty seriously lately. We didn't make it official, but I didn't want to. It felt weird because I still thought about Manny. But Manny was never coming back so I figured it was okay. They would fight over me all the time anyway. Ru was pressing on us being a thing a lot lately. He made me feel guilty about dating his cousin and said I owed him. Honestly, I felt like I did too.

In class today, all my classmates where talking about losing their virginity. It was something so cool and fascinating. Everyone thinks I have had sex and sometimes I feel like I did. I mean between fingers inside and penises being at the door but not being able to go in. I knew I was a fraud, but I didn't want anyone to think I was not experienced because I had plenty of experience. I may not have loss my virginity, but I knew a lot about sex, three play and more. Ru wanted me to come over after school and I made it my mission to go by myself. I told Taylee I had to stay after school for something, so she had to go home without me. She took the bus and I walked to Ru's.

We went in his basement, at first, we were catching up. His older brother came down before he went to work, and we talked. His brother claimed me as his best friend, and I thought he was hilarious. He told Ru I was pretty, and he said he was going to let us handle adult business. I've known about adult business since I was a child. He went up the stairs and out the side door. Ru asked if I wanted anything to eat and he made me pizza rolls. He came down, we played the game, ate and then he asked for a massage.

I hadn't given too many of those out, but I knew what a good massage felt like. People rubbed me up and down for so long it became easy. I got out the lotion, told him to take his shirt off and went in. I knew he liked it because he was groaning then I went in for the kill and gave him a hickey.

That is where it all went downhill. That was a turn on and he turned around and it got intense.

He kissed me, I kissed him back and before you knew it, he was in. It hurt so bad the first couple times but after a while those horse rides with Jordan paid off. That feeling I got with Jordan began to spring up in my body and I almost couldn't stop. Then Ru was done, and I was so disappointed. Not because it was done but that I did it. I wasted my once and lifetime chance to get it right the first time and nothing about it felt right. It felt good, don't get me wrong, but it wasn't enough. I was not done but it was. I wasted my virginity card. It wasn't special, it wasn't enticing, it was disappointing.

Ru didn't do anything wrong, I was just hurting inside. I also started replaying the memory I told myself as a child, "I will wait until I am married". Where was that memory at for the last four years? Why did that memory come back after I didn't wait? I was angry, I broke a promise with myself. I was angry I wanted more and couldn't get it the way I expected. I was angry that my first time was in someone's basement. I was angry.

That first time slip up, lead to more guilt, more slip ups, and more anger. Red loss who she was that day and she kept trying to find little Red, but she kept losing her. The cycle just continued to go around and round. It never seemed to slow down so that she could understand it either. Red and Ru engaged in sexual intimacy one more time and then she was done with him and herself. They were at a park in the slide when Ru pulled down Red's pants and had a quickie. Not the most enjoyable or even best scene but it was a wake-up call, RED get it together.

Red felt disgusted and she didn't know how to talk about the park. Most of the kids didn't go into too much detail about their experiences but just that they did it. She kept that park a secret up until a paragraph ago when you started reading. It wasn't her most pivotal moments, but she learned a thing or two about transparency.

Sometimes, it hurts to be transparent with people because we do not know how people will react. Sometimes we have more fear in healing than we do with staying damaged. The thing about transparency is that when you can be open about who you are, God can be open with his blessings. This book consists of a journey that involves hurt, shame, pain, up hills, joy and grace. Some of Red's darkest and untold secrets will be uncovered but they are shared to show people the power of transparency. Understand that you are not alone in this battle.

The things we go through, we often like to believe that we are the only people who have ever in the history of history experienced this level of affliction, shame or hurt. If by any chance you notice that some of these secrets are your own, I dare you to be transparent to yourself first and foremost. After you take the opportunity to acknowledge your secrets, I challenge you to find one person who you can trust. Not everyone is going to accept your secrets but find you someone (even if that person is the author of this book) that you can say I have this secret that is holding me back and I need to move forward. Don't allow shame to hold you back!

FORWARD THINKING

Telling a secret that you have held on to for years can be one of the most challenging things. Regardless if you feel like you can trust that person or not. It is hard enough to find people you feel like you can honestly open up to. Secrets are essentially messy, no matter how sweet, innocent or even painful they may be, there is a thin line between a secret and a lie. A lie doesn't always have to be something told to others it can be something told to ourselves.

Red has a theory about how we group our mess. There are three groups of secrets: Group 1, those we hold onto out of fear of judgment; Group 2, those we hold on to because it affects someone else; and Group 3, those we can tell. Red became a master at grouping her secrets and the park was one of them.

I was pretty ashamed with myself after the park, I am still not sure how on earth I allowed Ru to penetrate me in a slide. Men who love you have respect for you and there was no respect in that slide. I had gone in a spiral after that, I wasn't about to keep losing my own self-respect from men. So, I lost respect for them. I had made up in my mind that I was the player and I had serious game.

Me and Ru were extremely distant after the park, but I kept him around whenever I needed my ego boosted. Summer of 8th grade I was big pimping. Maybe I thought I had to prove myself because I was forced to go to this Early College (EC) Program next year and my friends were all going to Admiral King. I had one more summer to stay cool and make sure my friends remembered me. Regardless of how they remembered me, good or bad, I was not a lame and that was the most adventurous summer I have ever had.

I had a boy-toy who lived across the street from the middle school and I would go visit him some nights when I was supposed to be with Emma or Taylee. They covered for me all the time. He was at least 6 years older than me because he had his own apartment. Dear men, do not catch a charge for these little girls. Not every man is lucky enough to mess around with a little girl who chooses to be with them and not get caught with sexual predator charges.

The moment you turn 18, children under 18 should be out of your radar.

I would visit him whenever I was in the mood, but I played him more than anyone else. He just wasn't a Papi material. Although he was fine, he was too old to be intersecting with. We took naps together, we did a lot of foreplay but no sex for him. I was trying to save it for marriage, again. At least that is what I told some boys. They always tried to catch me off guard and slip one in.

Emma would call me if my mom asked about me and so would Taylee, that normally got me out of sticking around. I wouldn't feel so bad if I needed to go home so he didn't catch a case but if not I still did my one, two and left. Emma and I had gotten really close after Rosie threw her last party. I needed a home to go to and my mom liked Emma. She was the sweetie pie of our group so that's the home I went to. I didn't realize how amazing she was, and I loved her grandpa. He made us chicken before the party, and we got back super late.

He was down stairs when we came back from the party and he gave us a hug and went upstairs. We were thirsty and drank almost half of the bottle of long island iced tea. The problem was we really thought it was Tea. I had called Manny that night and told him how much I missed him, and he asked if I was drunk. My words might have slightly slurred, but I felt like I had it kind of not really maybe not together. He hung up on me and told me to stop drinking. Manny was so sweet he cared about me.

Emma called these boys who were beyond grown they had to be like 22 years old and they told us to come outside. Emma knew grown men and I thought she was the coolest because we just left the house and met them on the porch. I could never pull that off at my house. One of the grown men asked if I would talk to them in private, Emma stayed on the porch with Oldy and I left with Old Head. Then Grandad came out and Emma told them to leave and come back. It was the funniest night of my life, especially since we were drunk.

We finally came in that night and started watching American Best Dance Crew and that is when she became my ABDC. That was a thing for us for many years, we were closer than sisters, but we never called each other best friends, we had those already.

Red had changed a lot 8th grade summer, from pimping to drinking, she did a lot in a course of a few months. Her and Manny got closer again after that drunk phone call. Manny was probably trying to protect Red from going down a dark path. It could also be a direct connection with them being twerk buddies. Every party Manny wanted Red because they had chemistry in their movement. The world will never know why Red and Manny went back and forth in each other's lives.

When High School came around, Red was sad that she couldn't see her friends constantly, but she learned she could make friends pretty easily. ~&pretty had a white girl squad and most of them came with her to the EC Program. She also had a few other students who came from her middle school that she knew but none of them were her girls. She tried to stay inclusive with her friends by going to basketball and football games, but it seemed like the group became more and more distant.

Taylee met Yanna and had become close friends when Red went off to EC. Red felt like she was losing everyone and everything. She was dying again! Taylee tried to keep her involved in her new life whenever she could. Red hung out with Taylee and Yanna the most in the begging of 9th grade year. Red had also experienced her first family death since Great Gran. Charly's mom had passed away and although that was Red's grandma, she didn't really know her. Red felt more pain at the fact that she didn't know her than anything else. She remembered her homemade cooking and sweet potatoes pies during the holidays, but she missed all the fun grandma times.

Red was still big pimpin at the time, but this boy, Tate, caught her slipping. She was sad about her grandma and she agreed to date Tate and it was fine until Manny found out. Manny always got in the way of Red's relationships but this time Red genuinely did not want this one; she just felt sad and guilty, so she had to make someone feel better.

Never get yourself caught in a situation to make other people feel better, you can hurt yourself and them in the process. When new year's had came around Tate invited Red to a party, so her Taylee and Yanna went.

It was new year's and Mom had her own plans with my step dad. All Mom knew is that I was going to Taylee's. She had no idea we would be going out and kicking it. We packed our bags and headed over to Yanna's house. She was closer to all the action and her grandma didn't care what she did honestly. Not sure where Taylee's mom thought we were going but we were gone.

Yanna had major connections and got us some drinks before the party started. I am sure we were drunk before we even got there. We walked half silly to the party and when we got there we had more to drink. This is the party where I realized that being drunk didn't mean you don't know what is going on it means your not using your rational thought process. Did I tell you I kissed a girl? Yeah, that happened more than once that night. Tate wanted to kiss me, and I was more into the girl than him, it was a way out.

Then he kept pushing us to talk about our relationship. I was too much of a pimp to be tied down like this, so I asked the girls if they were ready to go. We were all ready to go home anyway so we headed that way fully drunk. Before we got there, we visited Manny, Ru and some other boy. Each house we got more drinks and I think I kissed Manny and

Ru. I have issues, why did I do that? Did I mention I kissed a girl?

They seen me drunk and they just assumed I was okay. We were still walking, and we met Gully and two other boys. I think they knew we were drunk too so they invited us to Gully's house. I thought this was the worse idea ever, but I was not going to walk home alone (my home was way too far to walk drunk) and I didn't want to end up at some boy's home. I could have called my mom but again no rational thoughts. Did I mention I kissed a girl?

We walked what seemed like half of Lorain to get to Gully's and I was tired by the time I got there. There were three boys, three girls and no adults. Taylee and Yanna went upstairs I was on the couch half sleep before I could even think. That third guy who didn't go upstairs with Taylee and Yanna stayed down stairs with me. He wanted to cuddle. I was fine with that until I started realizing why we were there. My first booty call, wow Red, how did you get here?

I was trying to sleep but my senses were off, and my sexual butterflies couldn't stop fluttering. I finally gave in and he went in. It was the worse drunk sex ever. I don't know how that is supposed to be, but it was horrible. I thought I had been disappointed sober; this was just shameful. I went to sleep after that because I could not boost this boy's ego up.

When I woke up, Gully's Dad was there looking at me half naked eating a bowl of cereal and said good morning. Yeah, that, what the heck reaction you just did, that was me. I can't believe I did that, he did that, and I kissed a girl. I woke up, threw my clothes on, ran upstairs and told them negros to get up. It was like 9 a.m. my phone was dead, and I knew I was in trouble. We walked back to Yanna's house and everyone had laughed except for me. I was so done with these two.

Red had a wake up call that morning, not everyone who is with you is for you. She didn't get caught but she punished herself. She couldn't understand how she allowed that to happen. She was aware of what was happening, but her impulses were stronger. Taylee and Yanna had told Manny and my oh my was Red over the lectures. She beat herself up and now Manny wanted to burn her with her mistakes. Red never understood how boys could do the same thing and it would all pass over.

I could tell Manny cared but why was he that mad. Me and him weren't dating and I had cheated on Tate, not him. He wasn't even mad at Taylee and Yanna, just me. I was the one to blame and I was over everybody. I kept my distance from Taylee and Yanna after that because I felt like they marked me as the bad guy, like it was my fault we all messed up. I am sure they had nothing to do with it but I think that was God's way of separating us.

I told Tate because although I was big pimpin I was not a liar. I just couldn't hold back on people like that. I thought for sure, that although I would've wished I didn't do that it was a perfect time for Tate to break up with me. I didn't know how to break up with people, it hurt too much. CAN YOU BELIEVE THAT DIDN'T WORK? Tate still wanted to stay in a relationship and work it out. He forgave me and I just had to let him down because I didn't want to be in a relationship. There is always a way out of mess but it's not always the easiest.

Although I broke up with Tate he showed me something that day. He showed me compassion and he gave me a second chance. Something I was not used to seeing or feeling. I felt like I was a failure at everything, and everyone made me feel bad when they knew my truths. Because Tate did not to give up on me he sparked something in me.

God will do that often; he will see you for exactly who you are and still show you love. He will continue to grace you and open up doors when you feel like you don't even deserve it. He see's who you truly are not just who you have been or who the world has made you. God wants to mold you; he wants to brake down the person you think you are, to bring you to who you have always been. That moment broke Red and change her entire direction in life.

EC made us take up this class with The LCADA Way (Recovery Program) we were talking about addictions and how dangerous they are. I didn't pay attention much in church, but I remember my Apostle talking about the warning always comes before destruction, so I went cold turkey sober. I was terrified to drink because I lacked the control over my body to stop that day. I always think back to that day because I could have died. I could have OD, I could have caught a disease, I could have been pregnant and for some reason God kept blocking things for me. That wasn't my first experience of drinking, but it was my wake-up call.

It's easy to take the little things for granted. To go through life and not realize how much God has shielded you from you. We like to magnify the issues in our life, the rape, the molestation, the abandonment, the homelessness but we forget to acknowledge that were still alive. That we could be some where far worse off then where we are. This is why it is so vital to tell your story.

Your story can be the story that heals someone else. Your story could be worse than someone else's and better than others. That is not to say that we have rankings when it comes to our pain and mistakes. Everyone's story is measured by what they can handle. Have you heard of that saying, "God won't put more on you than you can bear." It has more power than you could ever think.

I dare you to change your mind about your history, your current situation, and your future. Next time you find yourself wondering, "*WHY GOD, WHY ME?*" think about the fact that He choose you for this very obstacle because he knew you would overcome it. Think about the fact that he saw you for who you were and not what you were in. Think about the fact that at the end of the day you already won. Whatever battle is trying to stop you, God knew you would win, therefor forecasting that you have won.

Remind yourself that your past doesn't own you it owes you. When you deal with things that most people could not handle, once you make it through, and you will make it through, you realize exactly why you dealt with it in the first place. Unfortunately, a lot of our own cycles are someone else's as well and when we break free so can someone else. That's right, you suffer for your niece, child or brother/sister in Christ not too.

The sexual abuse that you suffered owes you a book. The domestic violence you dealt with owes you a platform. The job that fired you owes you a business plan. The miscarriage you suffered owes you the ability to love more. There are things we suffer, and they become hidden treasures in our story. They are the gems that keep us from turning back and the spark that keeps our flame. Don't allow disappointments to confuse God's love for you.

I think God was tired of me by the time I hit 10th grade. He took away all of my friends from middle school. Taylee had moved to Cleveland, Emma and I had a big fight last summer, I was done with Yanna from New Year's, Ru was old news, and Manny stayed around in and out. Basketball games where weird unless I went with people from EC. I did have my bus friends. Literally everybody who lived in Lorain rode the bus to and from the EC Campus. I had no choice but to make friends with them. They were funny too, so it wasn't all bad.

I had a group of EC friends, we weren't calling shots, it wasn't a click, it was just a group of friends. There was Riah, Tasia, Raya and the others. Riah ended up being one of my closest friends, she was more like a daughter to me though. I felt very protective over her because she reminded me of me. Some of the poor choices I had made I wanted to prevent her from making. I didn't have it together, but I knew she deserved better. She ended up falling in love early and I couldn't stand that relationship. Tasia was my nerd, I think I ruined her too. She was so quiet and goofy when I met her and then I got to her know her and realized she was just as crazy as me. Raya was the oldest and she had her life together, but she was the funniest person I knew.

The others were just people that I called associates. I was pretty much well known in the EC family. Our graduating class was merely 100 people, people left but there was never anyone new that came into the program for our graduating class. They really did become a second family, and everybody knew everyone's name. We had to blend ourselves with College Students and that is when I discovered College boys.

College boys were different; they were smart, fine and OLDER! My mistake was engaging in their conversations.

My brother Biggs had so many friends that went to the college and I always thought they were cute. Apparently, they always thought I was cute too. It could be because I started filling out more in body shape, but I am going to go with the first one.

One of Biggs' friends invited me over to study with him after school. He was just a hop skip away from my bus stop and I was used to walking around for boys. I went over to his place and we were studying for all of one minute. He started kissing me and OMGolly those lips. I knew I was in trouble then my pimping tools were fading away. I fell in lust with Biggs' friend and I had more juice to brag about to my friends.

This boy was on everybody's list and because I knew him, I beat those other raggedy scallywags! I continued my cycle and forgot about my marriage pretext. I had to put that one on my score list: yes, I was not the normal girl. Or at least the girl most people assumed I was. This went on for a full week until I had gotten bored and met more college boys.

There was Dimples, who stole all my sexual attention in the matter of a smile. He played on the basketball team, had his own apartment, and had hazel eyes. Who says no to a guy like that? I couldn't resist and I was hoping someone was praying for me because I couldn't think about anything else other than making him my main score. He was a daddy though and I think still in love with his baby mom. I was just a score for him too. I was more than okay with that at that moment in my life.

I really don't want to run you through all of my college men, but I just need you to see what happens when you don't deal with your own demons. At the age of 16, I had lost myself completely. There are somethings I had learned to deal with, but I was still carrying my bag of milky ways. When I entered this world, I just wanted to know who mommy and daddy voice was. By the time I entered 11th grade I had long replaced their voice with the voice of fear, shame, pain, hurt, sexual abuse, damage, anger, and brokenness.

VOICES

I heard voices all the time, voices that weren't even mine. I had a hard time dealing with those voices, but I knew something wasn't right. I remember asking my Momma if I could go to counseling and she kept saying that I didn't need it. She probably thought I was playing or I was not serious. I always tried to joke like my sister Mari, it made me feel better because she was the comical jokester out of my family, but this time I was serious.

Red really couldn't blame Charly because no one really understood that cry that ran rapid throughout Red's family. Red thought maybe Charly would see who Red had become but she had no idea. Red started feeling dirty about having sex and tried to distance herself from people. She felt like no one understood and due to the relationships she got involved in, she was convinced friends were not needed. Red was trying to redevelop her relationship with God and to make sense of the pulling feeling she was getting at church. The feelings that would tug her heart every alter call, the feeling that the Pastor was talking about her every trip, the feeling that her heart would drop if she didn't move in worship.

I never stopped going to church, I tried to participate during dance rehearsals and praise dance when I could. I started understanding the word of God more, but I wasn't really applying what my Apostle was saying. I was beginning to be convicted more but I still didn't know what to do with it. I felt bad about everything I did but I had no idea why. When I messed up, I didn't know who to talk to because everyone else seemed to have it together or they thought I was innocent.

I felt like people thought I was this perfect angel, like they put me on a pedestal to do no wrong and they wouldn't understand if I told them I messed up. So, I kept some secrets out of fear. That's my group 1 of secrets: the issues that no one else could ever understand. The issues that if someone knew I would be judged and never looked at as a human being again. The issues that hurt me the most but could never be spoken on.

So, I avoided my secrets and held on to them as long as I could. I brung my secrets in every relationship and told myself I would die with some of them. I would hide my dark truths behind a smile and burry them in other issues that didn't seem as bad. I would hide behind men thinking that it would help me get through the pain. I would self-medicate myself with the lust of my flesh because I didn't think God could really handle all of my issues. I didn't realize that if I would have just put it in his hands I would have avoided so many of my next steps.

Red and Manny had rekindled, and they were pretty serious this time around. Their bond was irreplaceable, but it had become toxic at this point. They knew each other like the back of their own hands. Their families were pretty well aware of them and accepted them for what they were "puppy love". That was huge considering Charly's last interrogation with him. Manny had moved out of the state a few times and they had some long distant relationship times but when they rekindled, they sparked dangerous flames. Flames that could have led into a gas tank.

Have you ever been so in love with someone that you don't realize the flaws in that person or the damage they have done to you? That's how I was with Manny. He had been practically the longest friendship I had ever had, and he knew me so well. He scared me sometimes though because the closer we got the more I had to push people away. I was studying for exam once and I couldn't check my phone during the practice exam. He called me 20 times, accused me of cheating and cussed me out. But somehow, I took that as he really loves me.

I loved Manny but he overreacted in ways that I was afraid to make him mad. I had seen him spiraling and I would suggest that we take breaks. He had some serious parental issues that he had to deal with that I couldn't help him with, and he almost ran us off the road arguing with his parents once. I saw how he communicated with his parents and it would rub off on our relationship from time to time. I was never scared that he would hurt me on purpose, but I had genuine fear that he was not mentally where he needed to be. I knew him though and I knew his story, he had every right to act out.

I realized we really needed a break when he started threatening to kill himself if we broke up. I would stay in fear for his life, but I knew deep inside time was sliding away for us. I couldn't really leave though because I loved him too much and I absolutely did not want him to hurt himself, I just wanted us to grow. When he finally broke up with me because his counselor suggested he should, I was happy for us. I should've listened like my best friend Dre when he told me to let him be, but I had to stay in contact.

Manny wasn't the only one to blame in our relationship. I cheated once and he knew the real me. I wouldn't trust me either if I was him. I try not to cheat because I am like I an open book and I can't keep water. I knew I was I was going to tell him and I couldn't stop crying because I actually wanted this relationship to work. Now granted my version of cheating was a kiss and some touching but I knew better regardless.

Remember when I said God will send warning before destruction. Red was on her way to a normal day of class and the teachers reminded her there was a special speaker coming in to share her story. She was well known throughout the media for something tragic that had happened to her a few years ago. During her junior year of high school, her boyfriend had shot her in the face with a shot gun when she had made up in her mind that she was ready to go. She almost lost her life that day and testified the miracle that she was. She struggled with insecurities about going from a pretty face to a now reformed face she had to learn to call beautiful. She went to prom the next year and eventually married the love of her life. Now she travels the world encouraging people to realize the signs of domestic violence.

How far will you allow someone to destroy you? This is not shaming or blaming the victim but at what point do we stop to notice the signs. How much is our life really worth? When you come into the grips that you deserve better, that you have more to offer, you have to make up in your mind that you can't continue doing what you're doing and trust that God will get you out of it alive.

Red never thought that Manny would actually hurt her but something in her jumped that day. She knew she had to cut off Manny. They were going to hurt each other more than they could ever build each other. They weren't growing together they were destroying each other. The following Sunday, Red learned about the rebuilding of the wall of Jericho in the bible. For some reason, she felt like her Apostle was snooping in her business. Like he was telling her that if she went back to rebuild the wall of Jericho, to rebuild the relationship with Manny, God will turn his cheek when he destroys it. That this rebuilding was going to be the very thing that ended Red.

Red heard everything clear as day. For one moment, Red only heard the voice of her Apostle. She couldn't hear the anxiety of not having anyone, the shame of being alone, or the fear of Manny losing his life. She couldn't stop crying and went up for prayer because she felt like she needed help making that decision. She felt like she needed strength to get rid of Manny. She knew it had to be done, she was willing to do it, but she had no idea how it would be done.

When she finally let go of Manny, she was depressed for weeks but she tried to walk around with a smile. She replaced Manny with college boys and work. She had gotten her first job around this time. She was on top of the world, making money and buying her own stuff. She had learned the principle of tithing very early on. She recognized that receiving the job had to be God ordained. She applied everywhere and yet she could not get a job.

Walking in the local mall one day, she went to Penny's Pretzel shop and asked jokingly if they were hiring, set up an interview that day and got hired immediately after words. She didn't go through a special program or even fill out an application. God literally worked Red's job out and it was one of the first building blocks to establishing Red's character. Red learned compassion and her joy for up selling.

Penny's also helped Red realize that she wanted more. There were some moments while she was working, she felt beyond belittled but she knew she needed money. Imagine being one of the few fully African American workers on a slow business day assigned to cleaning the creeks in the floors with a tooth brush. Red thought for sure it was time to quite after that moment, but she learned to endure foolishness.

Being at work, it took her mind off of other issues in Red's life and she really loved pretzels. It also allowed Red to see the benefits of earned income. She knew Penny's was not her permanent place of employment, she knew she had a future beyond where she was. She understood that she was going to be something one day so she dealt with it so that she can enjoy being able to afford things. Although she was not blocked from people, she could focus on her education and work instead of boy dramas.

Charly and Leo were excited that Red had a job. She could stop asking for money as much because Red understood she still needed her parents. Leo always tried to support Red though, because he understood that it cost to support a child. He wasn't on child support, but he avoided putting money in Charly's hand. Red hadn't realized why Leo was so against giving Charly money until Red made money herself.

I was sitting at the bank, setting up a bank account because I had money from my job with my mommy. They told me that no one beyond me, not even my mother, could take money out of the account but people could put money in. I was okay with that because I liked people giving money but taking money was a problem. I paid my tithes but overall, I was selfish when it came to money.

My dad taught me early on to tell my mom I didn't have any money, regardless of the fact that I had money. My mom would ask me to help out from time to time on very minor things or if she could borrow money and it would be like pulling teeth to release money from my pockets. I had goals and travel experience to save up for.

I was at school one day when I tried to order food at the cafeteria. It was right before class and I was starving so I ordered the French toast and eggs combo. I went to pay for my meal and my card was declining. Mind you there are people and friends behind me looking at me strange and finally the woman who was handling purchases told me I was fine. Since I was a regular, she said to pay her back later. I could not understand that because I didn't spend my money unless I needed to. I had more money saved than most people in my family.

I had learned to spend 10% and save 90% but I didn't have a separate bank account. I was flipping out and then I checked my online bank account. Apparently, I had spent all of my money at the Cleveland Jacks. I hadn't been in Cleveland in a while and I don't even know what Jacks is. When I realized it was a casino, I was calling the bank wondering how a minor can make a purchase at a casino and they said a withdraw was made by Charly. I FLIPPED! I thought these idiots said she couldn't take money out.

The bank insisted on telling me that she had access to my account, and she had privileges to make those decisions. I felt lied to, I felt betrayed and the only person I wanted to pay me back was the banks. When I addressed my mother, I already knew the reaction I was going to get from Charly. I call her by her whole name when she is under my skin or if she is trying to ignore me. Probably not the best method of having a respectable conversation. She shrugged it off like it wasn't a big deal that I had $1.17 left to my name, but I was furious. I couldn't do anything considering that was legally my mom, so I washed my hand with my anger, and I learned my lesson.

I wouldn't suggest ignoring your duty to respect your parents. I did it and each time it's like God got me. I thought because my mother was obviously wrong that God could make an exception for this case. Even in the midst of my mother being wrong, me being disrespectful, calling her by her full name out of spite was not the correct response. I only made things worse in the process.

Charly had her own demons she had to deal with, and Red didn't feel like dealing with them. Charly had suffered a lot of the same things Red had dealt with, which causes those generational curses to continue to cycle. Charly found gambling as an exit and Red would exhaust herself trying to understand why Charly did what she did. She was a loving mother and didn't mean any harm but Red was suffering because issues that were left undealt with.

I took all my money out of that account immediately; the entire $1.17 and then another account that Charly was attached too with a different bank, complete withdraw. I opened up with a bank close to my job so that if I ever needed to go during my break, I could walk over because I didn't have a car at the time. I didn't want Charly attached to anything money related, but I still wanted her as my mother.

It didn't matter how much Charly did to me I would defend her without even thinking. My dad couldn't say anything against her, and neither could anyone else. That was still my mom and I was the only one who could talk about her. My siblings shrugged it off when I wanted to talk about the betrayal, they told me to get in line. I guess it was normal and it was just my turn to get the short end of the stick.

By this time, I had lost most of my friendships and I was only close with Dre, Tasia and Riah. Raya was a come and go whenever I really needed to go places. I had my work friends, but we never really did anything together. I was still trying to be everyone's favorite and fit in with everyone, but I felt so distant from society. I felt like I had to watch my back and my heart. No one was incapable of harming me.

Me and my best friend Dre, didn't have to talk often but when we did it was like we never lost a beat. I had avoided him for a little while because he told me that he was in love with me. Have you ever been afraid to love someone who could have been great for you? That was me. I thought I would lose him like I lost everyone else if we went that route. So, I just pushed pass the simplest thought of dating him even though secretly I loved him to. I loved him more than a best friend, but I couldn't cross those lines. I needed stability and I was running away from harming it. A few months went by and I discovered I had too much going on and no one to talk to.

My best friend was my rock and he knew how to cheer me up. With everything that was going on with my mom and feeling alone, I had to reach back out. He was happy to hear from me and I was so excited to hear his voice. Instant joy rushed through me when he answered the phone. We talked for a few hours and then made plans to link up the following week. He talk about his new girl friend and I was happy for him, like the break was needed. Made me feel less bad about ignoring him but we joked about it anyway. He told me never to go that long again.

I was sleep when it all happened. When my mom woke me up in the midnight hour crying in an uncontrollable fear. She kept hugging me and telling me it was going to be okay. I couldn't understand what the problem was I had never seen my mom like this. She said it's Dre, he's dead, it's going... I couldn't hear anything else. I just sat there still in her arms, no tears, no feeling at all. I thought I must have been dreaming and I was waiting for that moment where I wake up from a horrible nightmare in a deep sweat.

Nothing was changing, she was still crying and hugging, and I didn't wake up yet. It couldn't be true, I had just talked him a few days ago. We had a date to go on, he wouldn't just leave me. I heard her speaking, but nothing was registering. She finally asked if I was okay, I heard that, and I asked her why. As if I had not been there and she said those words again, "He's dead..." I felt water hit my shoulder and I realized the tears had started falling. Then all of a sudden, they wouldn't stop, my heart had dropped in my lap and I felt like I was running out of oxygen. I had never lost someone I literally thought I would cross every major goal wit. I felt shame for taking so long to reach out. I felt weight for not telling him how I really felt and I felt lost because we had all these plans for our future.

Red managed to go to work that day, not really registering with her environment: she was sent home early. Then she went over to Dre's moms house and without any other words she just hugged her. It was the longest hug Red had given and the entire time his mom ensured Red that it was going to be okay. Red didn't understand how she could be so strong. She had lost her eldest son and had more strength than Red.

When it was time for the funeral Red thought, she had it together. It was one of the largest funerals Red had ever been to and she didn't understand why. Yes, Dre was widely known but she had heard so many people ridicule him and he had told her so many stories about how people were. She was angry that all those fake smiles were there but it was more of an escape from going up front to see the casket.

She sat down when she first got there until her mom asked if she wanted to go up. She mustered some strength to get up and start walking but she froze in the aisle looking at the casket because she never woke up. Red was hoping it was just some long drawn out nightmare, but it was real. She was losing breath and started to cry again, she couldn't go up and then Manny came to the rescue and helped her get to the front.

Seeing Dre in the casket, confirmed that it wasn't a dream. She was still trying to wake up. He had red and white on, his hair was in a box cut and he kind of had a smile on his face. He was always smiling. When they asked friends to come up and speak about him, I didn't feel right not saying anything. I talked about our competitions we had, the time he tried to push me into a truck, and all the goals I had to accomplish for us. It was the hardest thing I have ever had to do, and I can still see his face to this day.

That was the conclusion of my junior year basically. I had worked longer hours, studied harder, worked out to replace time and went to church. I was making it my mission to live for both of us. Keeping myself busy was just another way to avoid my true emotions. Deep down I cried every time I had some alone time. At night before bed, in the bathroom at work, in the back of the school bus in the morning, I was hurting. So, I tried to eliminate alone time and became afraid of it.

Going into my senior year, I discovered how far from reality I had been most of my life. We had moved again, that's 20 times in 16 years and I couldn't understand it. We moved to a small apartment that literally made no sense. My mom wasn't with my step dad anymore so I guess we were surviving but I was lost. She was trying to get her at home business up and running again and needed some help with a few items. I pitched in grudgingly because she made me feel horrible if I didn't. We were good here for a few months.

My brother Biggs had moved near us and I would visit him when I had nothing else to do. Emma had come back in my life. I think we grew up since the fight and realized how great we were together. She was like the sister I never had. She had a lot of things she was dealing with internally that I would try to be there for her with. We would argue but we didn't break up anymore. We would just walk away and call each other in a few days when the steam went down.

A few months into being comfortable at this apartment and we had moved again. This was my senior year. I was 17 years old and we had moved for the 21st time. Twice in one year, and I barely had things unpacked. I liked this house and so did Manny. I know, I thought God told me no already. Sometimes I didn't listen to my own instincts let alone the Lord's. We had stayed in contact after the funeral, he seemed different and plus it was around thanksgiving. I do not turn a free meal down.

My sister Marie, had moved back in with us and I knew this was going to be a problem house. Me and my sister didn't really get along unless we were in church. She was the one who showed me what being young and loving God looked like. Outside of those walls though, we just could not see eye to eye. Mom seemed to be okay in this new house at first and then I just stopped seeing her. I would go days without seeing mom sometimes and I didn't know why. I would blow her phone up and she would tell me not to worry. She would leave her car, so I tried to just take a road trip whenever I got in my feelings.

Red didn't know how to control her emotions during the 21st move she thought she was going crazy. Charly had started dating some man that Red absolutely hated, but she had no reason to actually hate him. She was always worried for her mom and no one else seemed to care. She felt like she wasn't old enough to just handle issues. Eviction notices would be on the door. Marie would tell Red it was time to start paying bills and Red had no idea where her mother was half the time.

Red would look forward to Sundays because everything went back to normal. Charly was home on Sunday mornings and off to church as a family. Charly was normal on Sundays; she would laugh and finally have a meal with Red. Sundays were the best and it seemed like everyone got along. The family was chasing perfection on Sunday mornings. No one knew what Red was dealing with Monday-Saturday and for the most part, Red was okay with that.

When the week started on Monday, Charly would leave with her boyfriend and Red would have the car. Red never had to worry about getting to and from work or even the weekly movie her and Emma committed themselves to. Red did miss her mom though and she would beg for her mom to stay home. Charly would say Red was being a baby and needed to grow up. Red and Charly had a huge argument one day and Red let all her Milky Ways out.

Red was screaming for attention and the need of having her mom there. She told her mom some truths about not being a virgin, and about not dealing with her constant molestation issues or the rapes in hopes that she would stay home more. That probably made things worse, to hear that your daughter has been suffering and you didn't know was a low blow. But Red felt lost for words and attempts.

Charly disappeared more after that until one day she broke down and started telling Red the truth. The truth about every man that had taken advantage of her, the truth about how she was hurting inside, and the truth about why she was running away. Red and Charly had made a promise to be more open and transparent with each other from that moment forth. They started packing for move 22 and Red was happy she didn't start unpacking.

They moved to a two-bedroom apartment with a swimming pool complex. It was a perfect move because it was the summertime and Red had something to do now. Charly still wasn't being quite honest with Red because she was still gone most of the time. Red was over trying to develop a relationship with her mother and focused on her relationship with Manny. (I know, she doesn't listen)

Manny would come and spend the night most nights and deep inside Red was hoping Charly would come home and flip. Nope, Charly just never came home and Red kept letting Manny creep in. Red really wanted to get in trouble more than anything and when it wasn't working, she started distancing herself from Manny. Those signs kept coming up with him constantly accusing Red of cheating. Red felt all around bad for entertaining Manny because she knew that this was going to lead to destruction.

I was hurt, Charly wasn't coming home, something in me was afraid for her life. I didn't know what was fully going on but she seemed scared about everything. I was sad and I wasn't in the mood for phone calls or people. Then my phone started blowing up, it was Manny. I ignored every single call until I heard a knock on the door. I was trying to act like I was sleep when I answered the door. He was drunk and emotional, I didn't have time for his mess. Tried to kick him out but that didn't work so I told him to sleep on the couch. I went in my room to read and he came in there to play. He was horny, I could tell by how aggressive he was with touching me.

I didn't want to do anything, the entire time me and Manny have known each other we have never had sex. I always tried to save him for marriage. I think Manny thought this was his shot, but I was not going for it. He knew where to touch me though, I won't lie about that, but I was serious. No meant no in that moment not yes keep going. When he started forcing me down and continuing his game I got stuck. I felt that instant fear of my 8 year old self and had no idea what was about to happen. I was terrified.

I pushed him off me and I was really hoping Charly would walk through those doors. I told him to sleep in my room and I was going to sleep on the couch. I knew he was drunk so I didn't want to put him out like that. I went to the couch and slept for all of 5 minutes when I felt his hands on my body, telling me scooch over. When I didn't listen that's when he just laid on top of me.

I told him I was serious, and I really didn't want to do anything. I had real fear in my heart and he finally caught on, she's not playing. I just laid there and prayed for hours until the morning had come. As soon as I seen sunlight, I kicked him out, figuring he was more sober he could drive himself home.

When Charly got home, I had tried to convince her again I needed her home by explaining Manny had almost raped me. Probably not the best of words because Manny would never actually hurt me but that didn't even help. I know me and Manny had a no meant yes kind of relationship, but I was wishing we didn't yesterday. Charly didn't believe me so I told her to call him. She did and that was a mistake.

I did explain to my mom that he didn't mean anything so her feelings of anger went away but Manny's entire family hated me. I guess they have every right too. Sometimes I make him out to be the bad guy when in reality I played a part too. In that moment, I really did have a flash back about who I was and not being able to defend myself. In that moment I didn't really see Manny, seen my best friend's brother, my cousin, my day care baby's dad, and so many more. I knew he didn't mean to but I hadn't gotten over any of my own issues.

GROWING UP

It was time to move again, 3rd time that year I didn't get it this time. Mom said she found a home that was better than the apartment, but I didn't feel like moving. I wanted to know what was really going on and why we were moving so much. I stopped unpacking at this point, so it wasn't a hard move. I was just devastated.

The house was a huge fixer upper. It was a two-floor duplex, but the landlord let us rent both units. It had potential and I could tell it made my mom happy, I just had no idea how we were going to do it. The front porch was dangerous, there were two attics and one had raccoons, there were so many windows that needed blinds and curtains, and the upstairs had a horrific smell like someone died.

We lived upstairs with that smell and she ran her daycare on the first floor. The good news, the smell only lingered when we opened the other attic door so we kept it close. There were two separate kitchens which meant we had to upgrade both. There was a parking lot attached to the house, but it was supposed to be shared next to this church. The church didn't speak much English, but they hated us. I couldn't understand why. We were so normal on Sundays and that was normally the only time we seen them. They put mud in my mother's gas tank once and her car had so many issues after that. At least we think they did.

I didn't really invite any of my friends to this house it was way too much going on. I didn't have any curtains in my room and most of our stuff was still in boxes 5 months later. I concluded that I wasn't rich at this house. My mom did a great job of providing and hiding the close to poverty line lifestyle, we were living but I finally seen it. I never did have all the cool stuff, but I never went a day without a meal. My clothes were decent, and I honestly thought we had some type of money growing up.

I stayed out of this house as much as possible. I only slept there but it was not my home. I was always with Riah, Tasia or some little college boy. I was not about to go home and deal with reality. I had my mom's car most of the time and I think she started to realize how much I had it. She was trying to stay home more often and watch her daycare kids so I figured she didn't need the car anymore than she did when she was always out with her boyfriend. I thought we were in a similar situation or I just really liked the idea of having her car. I think that was a mistake because she slowly slipped away again.

Sleeping at that huge house alone at night was some of the scariest nights I can remember having. Every floor creaked and the raccoons had a field day. I remember when I woke up one night and because I didn't have curtains or blinds, I looked out the window and noticed a raccoon family crawling on the side of the house to get to the attic. One of them looked at me and I just fell down like I didn't see a thing. As if I had just seen a criminal steal and didn't want them to know that I knew anything. That raccoon was staring at my soul.

Charly was doing better. Red could tell that she was trying to escape whatever she was in. Until one day, when the fan had hit the roof and the landlord served my mother a notice to show up in court for an eviction. Apparently, my mom had asked him to fix some things; the parking lot and the church and he refused to settle the empty promises that were made about the house so she withheld rent payments. When Charly got to court, she let the judge know she had the rent already and she would be willing to pay because she didn't have anywhere else to go but she would like for something to be done about the empty promises the landlord made.

The landlord had already made up in their mind that Red and Charly had two days to get out or everything they had would be thrown out. Charly couldn't convince the landlord anything different and out of stubbornness said fine. The court did not agree that the landlord had the rights to do so, but Charly knew she would never be able to stay there without constantly having to deal with the drama. It was becoming more of a tumbling block situation than building blocks.

This was move number 24 for Red who was just under 18 at the time. Red made sense of this one, she sincerely believed her mother was trying to make it work. She was nervous because they had no where to go and so much stuff to move. Charly and Red were moving into Marie's one-bedroom apartment and most of their stuff was going into a storage unit. Red could only take about 2 weeks of clothes and her essentials to her sisters house but she didn't think they would be there too long.

After about two months of wearing the same clothes, hardly seeing Charly and an overall depressed environment, Red knew things were about to get ugly. Red felt like Marie never really wanted them there, especially when she would walk in and go straight to her bedroom and lock the door. Red slept on the couch every night unless she spent the night at someone else's house during the weekend.

Marie was definitely not feeling us being there. I tried to make jokes or smile but that was hard. Between my mother who I could tell was lost and my sister who was struggling with something I didn't know what to do. I remember coming in from school once and Marie and mom were arguing. I stood at the door before I used the key to get in for a while. Marie was yelling at Charly about not being a mother and dealing with issues. That's when I thought I was going to flip. Apparently, most of my life is a repeat of my sisters too. From my mother, my sister and I, we have all dealt with tucking things under the rug when we were dying on the inside. That Milky Way bag has been passed along quite a few times.

What hurts the worst, is that my mother called Marie a liar. I know as black people we tend to think people are lying about issues that happen within the family. We like to blame the victim and expect each other to just get over it. That's when I walked in, and I tried to stop everything, but it made it all a little bit worse. That's when my mom stormed out and then my sister locked herself in the room. I sat in the living room in complete shock for hours. I was lost for words and actions.

My mom never came back after that argument she had with my sister, her stuff was there but she would only come grab a few things when Marie wasn't home. I tried to get them to talk it out again but I have a stubborn family. My mom was still my rock no matter how wrong I thought she was I couldn't seem to not want to help or be there for her.

She took me to work one day and I asked if I could have some money to pay for my graduation caps. We were bonding up until that point. I let her know my dad said he didn't have it and I really didn't want to ask granny for anything because she always did for me when they couldn't. My mom had a field day on my dad, she spoke about him like he was scum. I hated when they had issue with each other and expected me to speak for the other parent. I could tell my mom was hurting but I was carrying way too much weight, and this was not about to be added on.

I let her know that she should call him for any issues she had with him and she did not like my response. Then the words came out, "I wish I would've had that abortion... ". When I heard Charly say those words, I didn't see my mom anymore. I could barely see anything anymore my eyes were covered in tears. My vision was literally drowning away. I said some hateful things in that moment. I don't think she meant to hurt me the way she did, but I was beyond broken. Nobody else really seemed to trust my mom and honestly after that, I didn't trust Charly either. I felt like if she was pushing me away, she did a great job. So, I got out the car and went to work. I cut all contact off with my mom and I didn't expect to hear back from her.

The bible talks about Naomi and Ruth, how after Naomi had lost her husband and sons. She tried to go back to what she was comfortable with and push her daughters-in-law, Ruth and Orpah, away because she felt like she had nothing to offer. Sometimes people will push you away in hopes to protect you from them and the life they're headed to. I tried to be like Ruth and stick it out but those words rang through my head every time I got a call from Charly. For the first time, I heard Charly and I walked away like Orpah not even trying to look back.

When I got off, I went back to my sister's. No one was there so I had enough alone time to cry. I wrote a few poems in my book and then I went to finish some homework for school. Doing schoolwork seemed peaceful because I knew that was one thing I was good at. It also seemed to be the one thing that I could understand the outcome to. At that time nothing else made sense.

My sister walked into the apartment and it was like you could see the steam on top of her head. I thought for sure she was going in her room. I wiped my tears because I couldn't be seen as a punk but I wanted to cry out to her but she wasn't in the right space mentally. Instead of going to her room, she turned off the light I was using to study. She has never really been an open up kind of sister but what did the lights do to her?

I asked her if she could turn it back on because I was using it and she went in on me. I thought I might have actually done something wrong with having the light on for a minute when I realized she was just going through something. I had a bad case of sarcasm so I would laugh at people if they didn't make sense (BAD IDEA). She started telling me that I was inconsiderate and ungrateful and before I knew it she was in my face.

I knew it was time to leave and had no idea where I was going but I had to leave that situation. She must have wanted to argue with someone because she wouldn't just let me leave and that's when I swung on her. I had won a fight before, but I guess she knew she could just sit on me and shut me up. That's when I said some words I regret saying, words that hurt to the core and could ruin relationships. She finally got off of me and I walked out the apartment and walked over to my church mom, Gigi's house down the street. It was 1 a.m. she was the closest house and I knew she would answer.

She opened the door, I walked up the stairs, went in her room, threw the blankets over my head and cried myself to sleep. Geese I had no idea family was this complicated. I called my dad the next morning and told him what was going on. Gigi said I could stay there for a while and I was so grateful. It was a good thing I was on winter break at the time because Gigi had no way to get me back and forth from school.

My dad convinced me to call my Aunt T so I reached out and told her I needed somewhere to stay. I never would have in a million years thought to call her. I never really came to visit Aunt T or even thought she like me for that matter. I think I was used to being babied and she had no time to baby me. Aunt T wanted to know what was going on but I really didn't even know how to explain it. She let me come and live with her until I graduated from Early College.

Aunt T had a room with a futon and some space for my stuff in storage. I was able to get some stuff out of storage, but I had to convince the storage people and have my Gran pay them three months of storage rent. Apparently, Charly fell off the deep end and she stopped making payments. I could only get a few things because Aunt T didn't have that much space so I lost everything else after that payment my Gran made.

My Gran was always there for me she has been my best friend, my mother, my father and my spiritual inspiration. She always encouraged me to trust God's plan and to stay the course. She kept reminding me of different stories in the bible like Joseph. How his family turned their back on him, sold him into slavery and eventually he was the helper his family needed in hard times. She kept me sane most times.

I tried to stay calm but there was just so much going on before graduation. Charly would call and I wouldn't answer. School was winding down and I hadn't picked a school yet. I hadn't heard back from any scholarships and I was clearly over my head. My 18th birthday was around the corner and Charly wanted to plan me something. I thought I was walking into a church service because I had to dance. After I danced at this program, got dressed and came back all of my friends and family were there. I sat on the front row and heard stories from people encouraging me to stay the course. I was proud of Charly but I was still hurt from our last encounter. Plus it was Sunday, so I knew this high wasn't going to last.

On my actual 18th birthday I had gotten a call from someone I thought I was going to marry. He was older than me but I always thought he was perfect. He went to church sometimes and his mom was so nice to me. I think he was waiting until I turned 18 but he reached out and something was making since. We were talking for a few weeks and one night I had too much on my plate and he offered to come get me. I left my Aunt T's house and said I was going to a friends that weekend. He picked me up and we went pretty far out. He had the nicest car I had ever been in and I was so happy to see him. We were supposed to have a Netflix and chill weekend.

We defiantly watched Netflix but I am not sure how much of the movie we watch or the movie watched us. He was so cute and I was so vulnerable. I always wanted to know if he liked me and apparently, he did so this was an opportunity for me. All weekend it was me and him. Then he took me home so I could make it to church, and I had such a blast.

Unfortunately, my pastor was being nosey again and talking about me in the pull pit. I felt so bad and realized that he was not my husband. He was kind of a thug, he had seen people die, he didn't want people to know me because he had people chasing him, he was dangerous. I wanted to fix him and bring him back to the Lord but the Lord was telling me no. I tried to be friends and apparently that was not possible for him because he really loved me so I broke it down to him. We couldn't be anything.

I was still struggling when Monday rolled over and I realized I needed to get back and forth to school. I started asking 10 people a day for rides to school and then I forgot I had to work. I was paying anywhere between $80-$200 in gas a week just to make sure everything was taken care of. I knew I had come too far to give up on my education and figured when that passed I would be stressed free.

Aunt T, taught me a few lessons about bills and made sure I paid something toward the water or electric bill each month and I also had to buy my own food. I use to think that maybe she didn't realize I was on the struggle bus but now I am so grateful for those lessons. That taught me a thing or two about budgeting and making sure I take care of essentials before nonessentials.

I cut back on social activity and spending in general when I moved in with Aunt T. I was saving for my car because I knew I needed it. When I finally saved $1,200 I told my gran and my dad and we headed over to the auction. I bought my first car for all of $900 and it was such a reliable transportation source. It got me from point A to B, never really had major issues, had the coldest AC for the summer (I could only run it for like 2 minutes before I got chills) and it was all mine. I was so excited. My life finally was starting to make sense.

It was prom season; I didn't have anyone to go with, but I knew I wanted to go especially because I could ride there in my car. It wasn't the cutest car or the newest probably an exact opposite of that description, but I owned it. If you went to ECHS you had two proms your home school and the EC campus prom. Emma went to my home school so I seen her at prom, but I was with my girls each trip. Riah had a a date but me and Tasia didn't. It was fun and I had a blast. I wouldn't take it back for the world because in that moment it just felt like my family was healing.

Charly wanted to be there, and I let her come see me but I still had some serious resentment toward what she said. Jesus was betrayed but he realized that the enemy will use those you love the most to test your faith. Jesus understood that sometimes you have to talk to the spirit behind a person rather than the person themselves. Charly was trying to turn a new leaf though, I could tell. She even started planning my graduation party. I was so terrified that she would let me down, but I kept praying that God was changing her ways.

GRADUATING MY
PROBLEMS

Red was happy her last few weeks of school. She was finally crossing that road that seemed to be so far away. She had chosen a school to go to, she was moving to Cleveland just incase the dorms didn't work, she transferred her job to Beachwood, and the graduation party seemed to be in motion. She had two caps to decorate, two ceremonies to learn, one degree and one diploma to hold. She always thought after graduation all of her worries would fall and she was almost there.

Unfortunately, Red was concerned about everything. Red couldn't be Orpah, she couldn't see herself just leaving Charly without looking back but she was having a hard time forgiving her. She wanted nothing more than to be one big happy family. But she knew it was virtually impossible because her mind overruled her heart. Her mind told her that people who love you don't say those words. Her mind told her that she did all she could to help Charly and it didn't get her anywhere. Her mind told her to give up.

My graduations had me on a high. I was in a happy space and did not want to come down. People were cheering, I had support, my life was moving forward finally. My family was in town for my party and it felt so good to see everyone in such a peaceful manner. The party was an all-white affair ; it was nice, I had fun, I had laughs, and smiled all night. I went to visit my best friend before I left, keep him updated on all the good news in my life. I really do miss him sometimes. I hate that I even think about giving up when he can't even try to keep going. He's six feet under, and here I am complaining.

The party was everything: friends, family, food and money. No one argued and everyone laughed. For a moment, I had my big family. When the party was finished, I stayed there for about two days before I headed over to my Grandma's house in Cleveland. She had a room for me, and I was so excited! I packed up what I did have, and I moved out of Aunt T's house. My dad, Leo, has his own moving business so we packed his truck then my car and left.

I was happy for a little while and I kept my smile on my face. I started work and the environment was completely different. They didn't have the same care as the other location, but I kept going because I thought it was would be beneficial and I needed the money and the opportunity to meet people. I didn't know anyone, and I hadn't started school yet.

Red wasn't feeling well one day and had to call off of work, she went to the doctors and they gave her a few days to recuperate from her fever. Leo, Gran, and Papa went out of town and wanted to know if Red wanted to tag along since she was off. Red said no, she said she wasn't feeling well. In all honestly, Red wasn't feeling anything. When they left, she went to sleep, woke up, stared at the ceiling and cried.

She couldn't understand why she was where she was mentally. She kept repeating the words of Charly and she realized she hated herself more than anything. To top it off, school was seeming more and more impossible. She didn't have money for school, she hadn't heard back from the dorms, she lost hope in what God had already promised her. She started feeling like she didn't really need to go back to school.

Then she heard the creeps in floor, the emptiness in the three-story home, and loneliness of no one being there. She heard her inner self crying out for help and yet no one could tell she was done. She started thinking about how unfair life had been; how many people took advantage of her, how she had lost the only person she could talk to and how she was just going to end up like her environment. There was no bright future for Red to imagine, there was no greener grass, her life was never going to change.

My grandma literally has everything in this house. It's like a collection bin full of survival tools and gadgets. I was laying down crying when something in me jumped out of bed but although I could see everything, I couldn't feel anything. It was as if I was floating. I didn't feel my feet touch the ground or even my body leave the bed. I seen it, all of it. I've seen the wall paper from the upstairs to the downstairs; the kitchen sink, the basement door, the darkness of the basement, the narrow stairs, I'd seen it. Seen the storage area in the basement with all of the tools. Seen my hands searching for a rope. I knew what I was doing but I didn't feel anything.

I knew the stairs where a perfect distance from the floor, that after I tied the rope around my neck, kicked off the supporting chair I would be gone! I knew she had to have a rope, she literally has everything, but I couldn't find it. I was angry. I was irritated. I even prayed that God would help me find that stupid rope, but I couldn't find it. That's when I felt it, the tears that touched my face. I knew that this was the perfect day to do it.

I wiped my tears and I was back numb. I was back to only seeing and I seen my mind spin with new ideas. I'd seen the knife in the kitchen upstairs, I'd seen my vision move rapidly to get to that knife, and I saw myself holding that knife in my hand, and my reflection in it. It wasn't me; it was my niece. My precious, baby girl, my innocent, sweet, caring niece. There she was staring back at me with a knife to her wrist and tears falling. I dropped that knife so quickly because in that moment I realized who I would be hurting.

Suicide is an easy way out, it's complicated but it makes so much since in that moment. Until you realize who is really being affected by your decisions. If I die, who will write the book? If I die who lets me niece know she can't go out the way I did? If I die, who else dies with me? Who wipes the tears from my families face as they blame themselves for my mistakes? Who watches over my nieces and nephews? Who pays for the funeral? Who has to come home and see blood stained floors and their dead child or grandchild? Who has to live with my decision, everyone else but me! Suicide is easy, it's also selfish because we do have people who love us. People who would help if they only knew that we needed.

So I picked up the knife, cleaned it and put in the sink as if nothing ever happened. I went up the stairs, got in my bed and cried myself to sleep. This time, my cry was out of gratefulness, I couldn't believe how amazing God was. He didn't let me find that rope and he let me see my niece. There are some people that don't get those chances and there gone. Not too many people know what happened to me and the fight I had to loose to stay alive.

Not too many people want to admit they attempted to kill themselves or that they have problems in general. But God wants to use your story to bless someone else. God wants to empower someone who is on the brink of giving up through our stories. God wants to use you through your hell, your mistakes, and your peace. You are still worth fighting for, never doubt that!

When I made up in mind I wouldn't be in the same place I was mentally, this week as next week I pushed myself to believe in me. When I allowed God to come into my heart and transform me my entire life began to change. I already knew God had great plans and it's okay for your vision to get a little foggy due to weather issues but don't stay in fog. Turn on your defrost of praise and get the windshield wipers of prayer activated.

I never stopped going to my home church even though I was 30 miles away. My home church was helping me, motivating me and allowed me to see things differently. I was growing and I was okay with whatever God was doing. Sometimes you have to be in peace with where you are, trusting that God will move when he see's you are ready to move.

Once I gave in to God, put away my selfish thoughts he began to change me like never before. He opened doors that seemed so shut closed. I started a new summer job and made more money than I could ever think of. I heard back from the dorms and was ready to move in and I had a job at the school waiting on me when I finished my summer job. Doors were flying open. He even blessed me with a boyfriend who was really sweet and taught me how all women should be treated.

He opened up relationships and taught Red the power of forgiveness. There were a lot of people Red was not ready to forgive. She had anger and resentment for so many issues she dealt with. She was angry with Charly, her best friends brother and all the men she had ever encountered; every lie she had been told, the wakeup call to poverty, she just couldn't see the purpose of forgiving people who didn't apologize or don't realize the harm that they cause.

I had accepted what had happened to me; but I didn't forgive those that did me wrong. I never asked for half of the things that happened to me in life. I never asked for a grown man to violate me like I was property. I never asked to be born in a world I wasn't wanted. I never asked for any of that, so how could God ask me to forgive anyone. That's when he broke it down. I don't deserve anything that he does for me. I still mess up and I hurt people who hurt me. I hurt people who didn't ask to be hurt. I make decisions that go against what God instructed me to do. Yet, time after time, he forgives me. He allows breadth to be in body even when I don't deserve it. I expect him to forgive me and forget that my mistakes even happened. Every time I mess up that is another stripe his son took for me. Every time I choose to not listen or be lazy that is another nail in his skin.

I have had so many mistakes in my life, mistakes of sleeping around, being lazy, trying out sexual desires for the same sex, false pregnancies, hate in my heart, bullying other people, the list goes on. Yet God still forgives me, he still chooses to keep me and protect me. The pain that I have caused he ignores out of love and I can't forgive someone after He, Jesus, continues to forgive me? I had to learn that everyone deserves to be forgiven, no matter how much pain they may have caused. If I can't forgive people how do I expect to be forgiven?

My Gran was still my everything, but I couldn't tell her what I did. I didn't tell anyone what had happened. I didn't want anyone worrying about me or thinking I am crazy. I didn't need the constant checks up and strange calls. I just wanted to make peace with what happened and move. It didn't hit me until years later when someone I went to high school with committed suicide. If the rumors where true, she seemed to be having some issues at home too. I thought she was going to be the next big star for Lorain. I thought she had so much potential and I couldn't imagine any reason why she would leave. Then I realized that's what someone could have been saying about me.

I was more so hurt because I felt like I should have been more honest about my situation. Maybe the light at the end of my tunnel would have been bright enough for the end of hers. We can't dim lights because its comfortable for us because someone else needs it to be lifesaving. Our testimonies are hope for so many people that they can fight through, that it truly won't always be like what it looks like. My life has been nothing short of crazy but I appreciate the story that I do have.

It took me a long time to appreciate the story God is writing before you but I wouldn't change it for the world. Before I went off to college, before God opened new doors and I walk into them, God had to change my entire perception and my attitude. He had to replace the anger with joy and passion. I had to move forward with my life and accept people for people. I remember one Sunday, I had went with my grandma to church and the Bishop broke my issues down so clear. Bishop has always been my bishop; my grandma's church was my home church until I turned 12. He made mention that if we accept people to be people then we wouldn't be so hurt when they let us down.

He talked about how God expects us to lean on him for trust not man because it is the natural man's flesh to act out. It is the natural man's flesh to hurt and harm sometimes without even knowing. Man alone is not perfect but through Christ we are all new creatures. So I came to the conclusion that everyone who hurt me was meant to. For one, it made me stronger and secondly, they were assigned to do what they did.

In the bible, with the story of Job, the enemy went and got permission for the things he did to Job. Job was wealthy and had everything he could ever need. God had so much faith that his servant would come out to the other side more victorious and stronger than ever. Job lost everything and he still managed to lift his hands. The enemy recognizes what it is that we love which is why he will use those things against us more.

I finally saw what he was doing with my mother, my family, my relationships. I said: I forgive them Lord for they know not what they have done. Jesus said the same thing when he hung on that cross defending us to the end. Bleeding and dying with every breathe he took. When he was breathing, he had to pick his body up each time and re-puncture his self with nails. Jesus knew that this was God's plan that he had to suffer because soon he would rise and all humanity would have the chance to be saved if only they believed in him.

Everything that happened to me was meant to happen to me. I had to lose people, I had to cry at night, I had to try to kill myself, I had to become this new creature. I had to redevelop myself and I had to forgive. God had literally remade me but I still carried my bag of Milky Ways.

SNEAK PEAK:

Red was pretty well known on campus; she had a good energy about herself most people couldn't really explain they just loved her presence. It probably had everything to do with the God she served. He changed her completely, her attitude was at a minimal low, her smile was at an all-time high, and her positivity was consistent. She hadn't been there for a year when God told her she didn't have to wait years upon years for her dreams to come true. She always wanted to go the Garden of Claude Mone't and to Paris, France. God opened the door.

Even when she thought it was too farfetched, God made it so incredibly simple and close to reach. She had to make a choice though to stay back home to get ordained, something she felt so passionate about or to go to France for this once and a lifetime opportunity. Kids like Red didn't go to France, let alone outside of the state. She had to take the opportunity because she would have regretted if she didn't. Plus, every door God opened pointed to France. When she got back she was ready to get ordained, so on fire for God and knew she had to keep moving forward. She had to tell the world how amazing God was that he took a little girl from Lorain, OH all the way to France. When she had spoken to another preacher, man kind began to discouraged her. He told her that people don't want to be ministers, they are chosen. As if Red's desire was not good enough to be a minister. So, she gave up on it and left it at that.

Imagine building a gigantic snow ball really close to the top of the hill, you take a moment to breathe and sit and you accidentally push the snowball down. Instead of running after it, you just watch as it grows bigger and bigger, falling down at a speed you can't run until it hits a tree and everything just vanishes into the air. When your tired from building sometimes you make foolish mistakes that should have been avoided. That's what's happens when you graduate your problems instead of graduating your truths.

Red was building that snowball and she watched it fall but that is a story for a different day and a different book. Learn to become honest with yourself and let people know when your struggling. There are things you should avoid if you know that you can. Be open with God about what you struggle with, trust me, you can't hide from him. He knows even when you think no one else does. He knew Adam and Eve messed up and he still gave them life. There are consequences that come when we don't listen as with anything else but don't be so ashamed that you don't go to God to talk it out. Don't give up on yourself or your purpose.